THE
CHRISTIAN HOME
in a
CHANGING WORLD

THE
CHRISTIAN HOME
in a
CHANGING WORLD

By

GENE A. GETZ

MOODY PRESS • CHICAGO

Portions of this book are reprinted from the author's
The Christian Home, a Moody Manna booklet (Chicago:
Moody Bible Institute, 1967).

The use of selected references from various versions of
the Bible in this publication does not necessarily imply
publisher endorsement of the versions in their entirety.

Printed in the United States of America

CONTENTS

5

1

THE FAMILY IN CRISIS

AT NO TIME in history has it been more important to regain or develop a correct perspective on the home than in today's world. There are many voices "crying in the wilderness." *Time* magazine reported,

> "America's families are in trouble—trouble so deep and pervasive as to threaten the future of our nation," declared a major report to last week's White House Conference on Children. "Can the family survive?" asks anthropologist Margaret Mead rhetorically. "Students in rebellion, the young people living in communes, unmarried couples living together call into question the very meaning and structure of the stable family unit as our society has known it." The family, says California psychologist Farson, "is now often without function. It is no longer necessarily the basic unit in our society."
>
> The crisis in the family has implications that extend far beyond the walls of the home. "No society has ever survived after its family life deteriorated," warns Dr. Paul Popenoe, founder of the American Institute of Family Relations. Harvard Professor Emeritus Carle Zimmerman has stated the most pessimistic view: "The extinction of

7

faith in the familistic system is identical with the move-
ments in Greece during the century following the Pelo-
ponnesian Wars, and in Rome from about A.D. 150. In
each case the change in the faith and belief in family sys-
tems was associated with rapid adoption of negative re-
production rates and with enormous crises in the very
civilizations themselves."[1]

Sociologists and psychologists who approach marriage
and family relationships from a purely naturalistic frame of
reference believe that this important social unit as we
know it today, has resulted from a process of evolution. To
them all the rules, regulations, and ideals set forth for successful family living have been ground out of the mill of
human experience. The theory is that the more we know
of man—his psychological makeup, his tensions, his concerns—the better we can solve family problems.

Consequently, never in the history of the human race
has there been more written on the subject of marriage and
family living. Never before has the home as a social unit
been the subject of so many scientific investigations. Marriage counselors are legion, and child guidance clinics are
on the increase. Knowing these things, apart from a realistic view of the world in which we live, would lead one to
believe that problems in the home must surely be decreas-
ing year by year as man discovers more and applies his
wisdom to our social ills.

But such is not the case! Dr. K. E. Appel and Dr. Martin
Goldberg both from the Department of Psychiatry in the
School of Medicine at the University of Pennsylvania, con-
tend that the American family is "in crisis." They give
several reasons.

First, they believe the family is fragmented—that its
members do not "hold together as a unit any longer than

1. *Time*, Dec. 28, 1970, p. 34.

circumstances compel them to do so." Second, they believe that today's family is rootless, with no "long sustained ties and traditions that stabilize as well as bind." They say also that every member of the family is to a certain extent "uncertain and/or unhappy with his role." Wives are not certain they really want to be wives and mothers, husbands are not sure they want to be husbands and fathers, and children are not given the opportunity to experience true child life. Then, too, "communication between family members tends to be sparse, strained, and static ridden," and with a breakdown in communications, comes a "deficiency in closeness or intimacy." Many of the responsibilities that used to belong to the home have been "usurped by other institutions in our culture"—the school, the Boy Scout troop, the club, and one might add, the church.[2]

Thus, those who have studied the family from a scientific point of view are the first to admit that the home is a disintegrating social unit in American society. They note with alarm the need for reform.

There is only one perspective that will enable men and women to find answers to the perplexing problems facing them in their married and family life. It is the biblical perspective. Apart from God's laws and principles as revealed in Scripture, there is no safe way to determine ultimate and enduring answers. In fact, it is in the Bible that man finds the most basic of all discoveries which provides him with the meaning he is searching for—new life itself! This new life in Christ not only gives meaning to individuals but in a special way provides purpose and resources for those who "have become one flesh."

This is basically a biblical study. It is distinctive from

2. K. E. Appel and Martin Goldberg, papers presented to the Second Annual Clergymen's Institute, Desplaines, Illinois, Feb. 3, 1965.

other books on the Christian home in that scriptural content itself has been used as the basic organizing structure. A variety of scriptural passages and references treating marriage and family life have been gleaned from both the Old and New Testaments and have been organized according to topics and special subjects.

It is hoped that this treatment of the Christian home will serve several purposes. First, it will provide the reader with a compilation, simple exposition, and application of a number of biblical texts having to do with marriage and family life. In addition, it will provide pastors and teachers with basic material for developing a series of messages and Bible lessons on the home. It will also serve as a basic guide for small group discussions, particularly for husbands and wives and fathers and mothers. Perhaps one of its greatest contributions will be as a series of studies for prospective homemakers.

FOR GROUP DISCUSSION AND INTERACTION

1. Why is the Christian home *not* exempt from the general disintegration that is taking place in society?
2. What are some of the most obvious ways that changes in society are affecting the Christian home?

THOUGHT STARTER

Following is a quotation from Frank E. Gaebelein's, *The Pattern of God's Truth*: "For Christian education, therefore, to adopt as its unifying principle Christ and the Bible means nothing short of the recognition that *all truth is God's truth*. It is no accident that St. Paul, setting before the Philippian church a charter for Christian thought, wrote: 'Finally, brethren, whatsoever things are true . . . think on these things.' He knew that Christian truth embraces all truth, and that nothing true is outside the scope of Christianity.

"Now the next step is where many have faltered. In all candor it must be admitted that much education called Christian has failed to see that this comprehensive fact of all truth being God's truth breaks down, on the one hand, the division of knowledge between secular and religious; and brings, on the other hand, every area of life and thought 'into captivity to the obedience of Christ,' to use the great Pauline phrase. To put it bluntly, we have been too prone to set up a false dichotomy in our thinking and thus in our education. We have rightly enthroned the Word of God as the ultimate criterion of truth; we have rightly given pre-eminence to the Lord Jesus Christ as the incarnation of the God of all truth. But at the same time we have fallen into the error of failing to see as clearly as we should that there are areas of truth not fully explicated in Scripture and that these, too, are part of God's truth. Thus we have made the misleading distinction between sacred and secular, forgetting that, as Cervantes said in one of those flashes of wisdom that punctuate the strange doings of Don Quixote, 'Where the truth is, in so far as it is truth, there God is.' "[3]

QUESTIONS

If "all truth is God's truth," how does a Christian determine what is true in the principles and ideas that lie outside the revealed Word of God, for example, in the field of psychology, sociology, and anthropology? No one will doubt that much truth has been discovered and revealed in various studies in these areas in the behavioral sciences.

3. Frank E. Gaebelein, *The Pattern of God's Truth* (Chicago: Moody, 1968), pp. 20-22.

The important question is How can the Christian discover what is truth?

How is this particularly applicable in determining guidelines and principles that relate to marriage and family life?

2

GOD'S PATTERN FOR A SUCCESSFUL MARRIAGE AND FAMILY LIFE

A. The First Marriage

And the Lord God said, It is not good that the man should be alone; I will make him an help meet for him. And out of the ground the Lord God formed every beast of the field, and every fowl of the air; and brought them unto Adam to see what he would call them: and whatsoever Adam called every living creature, that was the name thereof. And Adam gave names to all cattle, and to the fowl of the air, and to every beast of the field; but for Adam there was not found an help meet for him. And the Lord God caused a deep sleep to fall upon Adam, and he slept: and he took one of his ribs, and closed up the flesh instead thereof; and the rib, which the Lord God had taken from man, made he a woman, and brought her unto the man. And Adam said, This is now bone of my bones, and flesh of my flesh: she shall be called Woman because she was taken out of man. Therefore shall a man leave his father and his mother, and shall cleave unto his wife: and they shall be one flesh. And they were both naked, the man and his wife, and were not ashamed (Gen 2:18-25).

Though it is true that God did not plan for every individual to be married and rear children, His general plan for mankind *does* involve these relationships.

After the Lord God had created the first man, Adam, He said, "It is not good that the man should be alone; I will make him an help meet for him" (Gen 2:18). God had already given Adam a beautiful home, the Garden of Eden, which included "every tree that is pleasant to the sight, and good for food" (Gen 2:9). Adam was given the responsibility to "dress" the garden and "to keep it" (Gen 2:15). He was also given authority over all other earthly created beings and he named "every beast of the field, and every fowl of the air" (2:19). But in spite of all these benefits—natural beauty, sustenance, responsibility, authority, and above all, God's presence—Adam was still incomplete. He needed a human companion with whom he could fellowship and discover fullness.

When God said, "It is not *good* that man should be alone," He did not mean that what He had already created and provided for Adam was bad. He simply meant that Adam was incomplete without Eve. He needed a help meet with whom to share all his material and spiritual blessings. Unfortunately, "help meet" does not convey the full meaning of what God was saying. Woman was to be more than a "companion and helper," more than a help-*mate*. Rather, she was to be a "helper suited to Adam," or more literally, "a helper as his counterpart." This more clearly describes God's purpose in including woman in His plan for man. She was to be his counterpart, his complement, his equal.

Interestingly, Eve was taken out of Adam's side, not out of some lower or upper part of his body (2:21). Some believe this suggests her equality with man.

Notice that God brought Eve to Adam (2:22). The

Creator of the universe, the Lord of heaven, became the first person to "give away" a bride, His own daughter, the one He had perfectly designed. Thus God added His special blessing to this first marriage.

Adam recognized immediately the uniqueness of his new companion. She was more perfect than any other created being he had encountered heretofore. He perceived her unusual relationship to him and responded by saying, "This is now bone of *my* bones, and flesh of *my* flesh" (2:23). He claimed her as his very own.

B. A Divine Pattern

This scriptural record of the first marriage includes at least six principles which establish a divine pattern.

First, *the choice of a life mate should involve God.* Though man's will is involved in taking this important step, God's will is even more important. God's promise of guidance extends to all points of life. In Proverbs 3:5-6 we read: "Trust in the LORD with all thine heart; and lean not unto thine own understanding. In all thy ways acknowledge him, and he shall direct thy paths."

How important it is that God's direction be sought in deciding on a marriage partner!

Second, *marriage means companionship and unity.* It is a cooperative venture. Amos appropriately asks, "Can two walk together, except they be agreed?" (Amos 3:3). Applied to marriage, the answer to this question is decidedly no. Eve was created as Adam's counterpart, as his complement. Thus it is of supreme importance that there be unity of faith. To marry a nonbeliever is to ask for trouble. It violates a principle established in Eden.

Later, Moses, when instructing the children of Israel regarding marriage, gave explicit instructions regarding this important principle. Their daughters and sons were not to "make marriages" with the unbelieving people of the land (Deu 7:3). To do so would surely bring God's judgment, for the end result of such intermingling would be idolatry and utter spiritual failure.

Many years later, the apostle Paul, in writing to the Corinthian church, set forth a more general teaching, but one which applies directly to marriage. "Be ye not unequally yoked together with unbelievers: for what fellowship hath righteousness with unrighteousness? and what communion hath light with darkness?" (2 Co 6:14).

Today, more than ever before, it is important to take a serious look at these straightforward teachings from the Word of God. There is no question about it. God is displeased when Christians marry non-Christians. He does not and cannot add His sacred blessing to such a union.

In some instances, the unsaved mate later comes to Christ. But in far more cases, the home established under these conditions has become a place of heartache and disappointment. When a non-Christian mate refuses to show an interest in spiritual goals (which is natural), the Christian mate, in order to maintain a degree of unity, frequently becomes complacent about spiritual interests, and may even, as Moses warned, "turn away" from following God (Deu 7:4).

The emphasis in Deuteronomy 7:3 is significant, for God is speaking to parents. He warns them not to encourage their children to marry unbelievers. The spiritual lesson is clear! Christian parents should start early to teach their children the importance of marrying Christians. They must not wait until they are already dating the unsaved. The important principle of not being unequally yoked must be built into the child's moral and spiritual fiber early in life. To delay teaching this truth to children is to set the stage for heartache and sorrow. When they are teens, it may be too late.

Third, *marriage as originally planned involved one man and one woman.* Polygamy was not God's idea for successful marriage. Having more than one wife was introduced because of man's sinful nature, his own self-will, and his tendency to leave God out of his plans. Wherever it was practiced, it created problems that led to unhappiness, jealousy, and many other difficulties. A man is to be "one flesh" with *one* woman.

Fourth, *marriage involves physical union.* Since that first marriage, God's plan for husband and wife has included this important relationship (Gen 1:28; Pr 5:18-20). In some mysterious and wonderful way, it is the means whereby God says man and woman "become one flesh" (1 Co 6:15-16).

Fifth, *marriage involves a new social unit.* To be successfully married, both man and woman must leave father and mother and establish a new home (Gen 2:24). In fact, it is the parents' responsibility to help prepare their children for the time when they break home ties and establish a new dependency.

Sixth, *marriage is for keeps.* Though God says nothing specifically in Genesis 2:18-25 regarding the possibility of separation (sin had not yet entered the race), the term "shall cleave" strongly implies that this union was life-long. Jesus later clarified this: "What therefore God hath joined together, let not man put asunder" (Mt 19:6).

C. Marriage Not for All

Though it is important in God's plan for mankind, married as well as unmarried should know that marriage is not the most important relationship in life. Our relationship to God through Jesus Christ is far more significant. In fact, the Word of God teaches that marriage is not for everyone. Even Paul, who penned some of the most profound truths regarding the importance of marriage, may not himself have been married. He said, "I would that all men were even as I myself. . . . I say therefore to the unmarried and widows, It is good for them if they abide even as I" (1 Co 7:7-8).

Some people have falsely concluded that marriage is absolutely necessary for happiness. Nothing could be farther from the truth. Facts alone reveal that there are multiplied thousands who are married, some even among Christians, who wish they could be released from marital responsibility.

Those who marry in the will of God and live according to God's pattern for successful marriage, experience great blessing and happiness. Those who do not marry, but who are living in the will of God, can also experience just as much blessing and happiness. For married people, a great source of happiness naturally relates to their God-ordained environment in the home. For unmarried people, their source of contentment relates to numerous other environmental factors: their relationship to God, their independence from domestic responsibilities, their opportunity to be mobile and to engage in self-development. Perhaps most important, the unmarried person can engage in fulltime service for Jesus Christ without being concerned with family responsibilities (1 Co 7:32-34).

It is unfortunate when, particularly in Christian circles, there is criticism of the unmarried person. This is frequently done in the form of teasing but often creates deep feelings of hurt and anxiety. We must remember that one of the greatest problems faced by the single person is to accept his role in life in a society that is supercharged with "marriage consciousness." In America the expected pat-

tern of life is marriage. However, the Scriptures teach that
some are to remain unmarried to fulfill God's purposes in
a special way.

One outstanding illustration of a single woman called of
God to a life of fruitful service is the late Dr. Henrietta
Mears. Of her Dr. Billy Graham has said, "She has had a
remarkable influence, both directly and indirectly, on my
life. In fact, I doubt if any other woman outside of my
wife and mother has had such a marked influence. . . . She
is certainly one of the greatest Christians I have ever
known."[1]

Her influence was also significant in the life of Bill
Bright, founder of Campus Crusade for Christ. Bill was a
member of the college group she taught and it was in her
home that Campus Crusade was launched.

Under her dynamic leadership as director of Christian
education at the Hollywood Presbyterian Church, the
Sunday school enrollment grew from 450 to 4,200 in two
and one-half years—an average weekly gain of over thirty
people per Sunday. Out of the college class which she
taught, hundreds of young men were challenged to go into
the ministry. Furthermore, the Sunday school literature
written by Dr. Mears and her co-workers at the Hollywood
Church eventually became the material published by
Gospel Light Publications—a ministry which now circles
the globe.

But this outstanding and fruitful life was not without a
period of crisis in her younger days. She had many male
friends, but really loved only one—a person of a different
faith. When faced with tension and conflict about this
decision she turned to the Lord and prayed: "Lord, you
have made me the way I am. I love a home, I love security,
I love children, and I love him. Yet I feel that marriage

1. Billy Graham, Introduction to *The Henrietta Mears Story*, by Bar-
bara Hudson Powers (Westwood, N.J.: Revell, 1957), p. 7.

under these conditions would draw me away from You. I surrender even this, Lord, and leave it in your hands. Lead me, Lord, and strengthen me. You have promised to fulfill all my needs. I trust in you alone."[2]

After this prayer, the friendship was ended. Many years later as she looked back on this experience, Dr. Mears wrote: "The marvelous thing has been that the Lord has always given me a beautiful home; he has given me thousands of children; he has supplied every need in my life, and I've never felt lonely. Since I am a very gregarious person, I thought I would have a feeling I didn't belong. But I've never had it, never! I've never missed companionship. Through one experience after another the Lord has shown me that he had something special for me to do. After I went through that final door, where it was just the Lord and I, into wide open spaces of people and things and excitement, life has been one great adventure."[3]

FOR GROUP DISCUSSION AND INTERACTION

CASE STUDY

John and Mary, both Christians since childhood, dated for two years in college before they married. They had a relatively good relationship—enjoyed each other's company, found they had a lot in common, felt attracted to each other emotionally and physically, and finally decided they were in love. However, shortly after they were married, the satisfaction they had enjoyed prior to marriage began to wane. Now they're not as sure they were meant for each other. They have nagging doubts about their marriage. They are easily irritated with each other, and neither is as happy as they had anticipated they would be.

2. Ethel M. Baldwin and David V. Benson, *Henrietta Mears and How She Did It* (Glendale, Calif.: Gospel Light, Regal Books, 1966), pp. 42-43.

3. Ibid., p. 43.

1. What may be wrong in this relationship?
2. What suggestions would you give John and Mary if they came to you for counseling?

THE SINGLE ADULT

If marriage is not for all, what should the church be doing for the single adult?

3

THE CHRISTIAN HUSBAND

A. His Character

Submitting yourselves one to another in the fear of God. Wives, submit yourselves unto your own husbands, as unto the Lord. For the husband is the head of the wife, even as Christ is the head of the church: and he is the saviour of the body. Therefore as the church is subject unto Christ, so let the wives be to their husbands in everything. Husbands, love your wives, even as Christ also loved the church, and gave himself for it; . . . That he might present it to himself a glorious church, not having spot, or wrinkle, or any such thing; but that it should be holy and without blemish. So ought men to love their wives as their own bodies. He that loveth his wife loveth himself. For no man ever yet hated his own flesh; but nourisheth and cherisheth it, even as the Lord the church: For we are members of his body, of his flesh, and of his bones. For this cause shall a man leave his father and mother, and shall be joined unto his wife, and they two shall be one flesh. This is a great mystery: but I speak concerning Christ and the church. Nevertheless let every one of you in particular so love his wife even as himself;

and the wife see that she reverence her husband (Eph 5:21-33).

The Old Testament describes the first marriage, and sets forth general principles and guidelines for a successful relationship. The New Testament, however, develops more in detail the specific responsibilities of both husband and wife. Paul says in Ephesians 5:25, "Husbands, love your wives, even as *Christ* also *loved* the *church*, and gave himself for it." What kind of love is this? It is a love that can only be understood as Christ's relationship to the church is understood.

First, *Christ demonstrated a great spirit of unselfishness* (Phil 2:6). When He existed "in the form of God," He did not consider this position something to be "grasped" or "clutched" for personal pleasure. He was willing to lay aside His enjoyment of glory with the Father to come into this world to fulfill God's redemptive plan for man.

Second, *Christ demonstrated unusual humility* (Phil 2:7). Upon leaving the glories of heaven, He "made himself of no reputation"; He "took upon him the form of a servant"; He was made "in the likeness of men." He exchanged the ivory palaces for a stable and His sovereignty for servitude.

Third, *Christ sacrificed His very life* (Phil 2:8). He "became obedient unto death, even the death of the cross." He paid the supreme sacrifice and demonstrated the greatest act of love known to man (see Jn 15:13).

Fourth, *Christ prays and cares for His own* (Heb 4:14-16). After His death and resurrection, He "passed into the heavens" to become a great High Priest who can "be touched with the feeling of our infirmities." He stands ready to provide "mercy" and "grace to help in time of need."

Fifth, *Christ has an ultimate plan for the church* (1 Th 4:16-17). Someday He is coming to call His saints home to glory to live with Him forever.

This then is the pattern by which Paul exhorts husbands to love their wives. All Christians, of course, are to have the mind of Christ (Phil 2:5), but these specific characteristics of our Lord have special application to Christian husbands. When Paul said to "love as Christ loved" he implied (1) an unselfish attitude toward all aspects of the marriage relationship, (2) a spirit of humility and servitude, (3) a willingness to undergo great personal sacrifice, even to the point of death, (4) a deep concern for all her needs—spiritual, emotional, social, and physical, and (5) long-range planning that provides for her personal welfare and happiness.

The apostle Peter goes a step further in developing a criteria for evaluating the character of a Christian husband. "Likewise, ye husbands, dwell with them according to knowledge, giving honour unto the wife, as unto the weaker vessel, and as being heirs together of the grace of life; that your prayers be not hindered" (1 Pe 3:7). It is of utmost importance that a Christian husband *understands* his wife, that he recognize her limited stamina, and consequently give her proper consideration and protection. By contrast, however, he should recognize her spiritual equality, even though she may lack in physical equality. She shares equality in God's grace and His gift of eternal salvation. To downgrade her position in Christ is to violate clear scriptural teaching.

Of utmost importance? Yes, to be lacking in this awareness and to fail to apply this knowledge results, says Peter, in unanswered prayer. To fail to measure up to this important criteria will inevitably result in spiritual weakness and lack of power in the Christian life.

B. His Leadership Role

Though Eve was created as Adam's counterpart, it was God's plan that man was to be the head administrator in the home. Throughout Old Testament days, this was the pattern for governing family affairs. During New Testament times, this principle was reaffirmed and illustrated by Christ's relationship to the church.

In the Ephesians passage, Paul states: "The husband is the head of the wife, even as Christ is the head of the church" (5:23). Again he says, "But I would have you know, that the head of every man is Christ; and the head of the woman is the man; and the head of Christ is God" (1 Co 11:3). Paul reminds his readers that "the man is not of the woman; but the woman of the man. Neither was the man created for the woman; but the woman for the man" (vv. 8-9).

This biblical principle of administrative authority extends beyond the home. When writing to Timothy about proper procedures in the church, Paul gave specific instructions that women were not "to usurp authority over the man" (1 Ti 2:12). Wherever this principle is violated either in the home or church, problems usually result. "For Adam was first formed, then Eve" (1 Ti 2:13). This is the order for leadership.

Does this mean that wives have no freedom? Perhaps this can best be answered by posing another question: Since Christ is the Head of the church, does this mean that its members have no freedom? Not at all! The only really "free" people are children of God! As Christians, we are enjoined to "stand fast therefore in the liberty wherewith Christ hath made us free" (Gal 5:1).

But wait! Is this not a contradiction? Is not the Christian a bond slave of Jesus Christ? How can one be a slave and yet free? The answer is found in understanding the nature of the divine relationship which exists between Christ and each of His true children. Jesus said, "He that loseth his life for my sake shall find it" (Mt 10:39). Just so, where a husband exercises his headship by following Christ's example, a wife who submits to this Christ-like headship as the church is subject to Christ, will discover freedom and happiness.

FOR GROUP DISCUSSION AND INTERACTION

Study carefully 1 Peter 3:7. The apostle Peter instructs husbands to dwell with their wives "according to knowledge."

1. What should a husband know about his wife to be able to fulfill this imperative?
2. What does this verse have to say about the Women's Liberation movement?
3. What are the profound implications of the words "that your prayers be not hindered"?

4

THE CHRISTIAN WIFE

A. Her Role

> Likewise, ye wives, be in subjection to your own husbands; that, if any obey not the word, they also may without the word be won by the conversation of the wives; While they behold your chaste conversation coupled with fear. Whose adorning let it not be that outward adorning of plaiting the hair, and of wearing of gold, or of putting on of apparel; But let it be the hidden man of the heart, in that which is not corruptible, even the ornament of a meek and quiet spirit, which is in the sight of God of great price. For after this manner in the old time the holy women also, who trusted in God, adorned themselves, being in subjection unto their own husbands: Even as Sarah obeyed Abraham, calling him lord: whose daughters we are, as long as ye do well, and are not afraid with any amazement (1 Pe 3:1-6).

Since the husband is to be the head of the wife just as Christ is the head of the church, it follows naturally that the wife is to be subject to Christ (Eph 5:24). Ephesians 5:22 says, "Wives, submit yourselves unto your own husbands, as unto the Lord." Husbands are to love their wives as Christ loved the church, and wives are to submit to their husbands as the church is to submit to Christ.

One of the most comprehensive teachings regarding every Christian's responsibility to submit to Christ is found in Romans 12:1-2. Here we are requested to present ourselves unto God "a living sacrifice." We are not to be "conformed to this world" but to be "transformed." Every believer who daily experiences this type of relationship with Christ knows that this is the secret to victorious living and to proving step-by-step the "good, and acceptable, and perfect, will of God."

From this important passage about the church's relationship to Christ, one can gain an important principle which helps explain Paul's words in Ephesians 5:22-24. For the wife to submit to her husband as the church submits to Christ means total dedication.

This type of loyalty need not interfere with a wife's dedication to Christ. At this point her dedication on the human level blends so completely with her dedication to Christ that the two merge into one.

It is true that the Bible pictures marriage as a foretaste of heaven. However, we must recognize that there is no perfect human relationship. As long as we are in this world and subject to sin, there will be failures, difficulties and troubles. But as a husband becomes more conformed to the image of Christ in his love, and as a wife becomes more submissive to her husband, their relationship will become richer and more satisfying. Remember that this results only when both partners fulfill their roles. It is not fair for a Christian husband to demand submission from his wife when he himself is not Christ-like toward her. True love and respect cannot be demanded; they are won through consistent Christian behavior toward the object loved.

B. Her Significant Contributions

If you can find a truly good wife, she is worth more than precious gems! Her husband can trust her, and she will richly satisfy his needs. She will not hinder him, but help him all her life. She finds wool and flax and busily spins it. She buys imported foods, brought by ship from distant ports. She gets up before dawn to prepare breakfast for her household, and plans the day's work for her servant girls. She goes out to inspect a field, and buys it; with her own hands she plants a vineyard. She is energetic, a hard worker, and watches for bargains. She works far into the night! She sews for the poor, and generously gives to the needy. She has no fear of winter for her household, for she has made warm clothes for all of them. She also upholsters with finest tapestry; her own clothing is beautifully made—a purple gown of pure linen. Her husband is well known, for he sits in the council chamber with the other civic leaders. She makes belted linen garments to sell to the merchants. She is a woman of strength and dignity, and has no fear of old age. When she speaks, her words are wise, and kindness is the rule for everything she says. She watches carefully all that goes on throughout her household, and is never lazy. Her children stand and bless her; so does her husband. He praises her with these words: "There are many fine women in the world, but you are the best of them all!" Charm can be deceptive and beauty doesn't last, but a woman who fears and reverences God shall be greatly praised. Praise her for the many fine things she does. These good deeds of hers shall bring her honor and recognition from even the leaders of the nations (Pr 31:10-31, *Living Psalms and Proverbs*).

It has often been said that behind every great man stands a great woman. It is not true, of course, that only married men become successful. The apostle Paul, for example, may never have been married, but all will agree that he was very successful.

But it is true that married men are greatly dependent on their wives. The Word of God says that "a virtuous woman is a crown to her husband" and "her price is far above rubies" (Pr 12:4; 31:10). The modern definition of virtuous does not do justice to the original meaning which implies "strength and worth."

A woman of this caliber, one who loves her husband, who is dedicated to him, who is subject to him as the church is subject to Christ, "will do him good and not evil all the days of her life" (Pr 31:12). She who faithfully cares for her household responsibilities (vv. 15-22), who fulfills her God-ordained role, not only contributes to her own happiness (v. 28) but also to her husband's success (v. 23).

When one thinks of great Christian leaders of the past century, D. L. Moody stands out. His accomplishments were unusual, and the results of his efforts, rather than diminishing at his death, have grown and multiplied to reach around the world, particularly through the outreach of Moody Bible Institute. Yet, one seldom hears of Moody's wife.

If D. L. Moody were alive today, he would no doubt be the first to give her credit. In fact, he would probably relate an incident that took place in 1887. He became so discouraged because of multiplied problems surrounding the newly formed Chicago Evangelization Society that he resigned. But Mrs. Moody encouraged him to withdraw his resignation and to take up the reins of leadership. That organization eventually became Moody Bible Institute. Humanly speaking, there may have been no institute apart from a woman who stood behind a man and encouraged him when he needed it most.

Yes, woman was made for man! Why? Because God knew he needed her (Gen 2:18).

C. Her Spiritual and Emotional Development

In writing to Titus, Paul instructs him to teach the older women "to be reverent in their behavior, not malicious gossips, nor enslaved to much wine, teaching what is good, that they may encourage the young women to love their husbands, to love their children, to be sensible, pure, workers at home, kind, being subject to their own husbands, that the word of God may not be dishonored" (Titus 2:3-5, NASB[1]).

The older women were to be reverent in their behavior and were not to be malicious gossips or slaves to drink. They were to teach what is good and to soberly encourage the younger women by godly example and advise them of their responsibilities in the home.

The younger women were first *"to love their husbands."* In other passages of Scripture wives are told to submit to the authority of their husbands. Here, however, they are to be taught to "love their husbands." True respect, submission, and reverence can only grow out of love. And, interestingly, Paul implies that love can be taught. Where it is weak, it can be developed by the power and presence of the Holy Spirit (Gal 5:22).

Second, they were *"to love their children."* Some have proposed that a mother's love for her baby is natural, innate, and automatic. If this is true, we are hard put to explain "doorstep babies," abortions, and other similar occurrences that do not reflect love.

The truth is that experiments by psychologists have shown that some animals have more innate attachments for their young than human beings. Shocking but true! The

1. New American Standard Bible.

human heart has been spoiled by sin; and love must be learned, developed, and quickened by the Spirit of God.

Third, they were *"to be sensible, pure, workers at home, kind, being subject to their own husbands."* These descriptive words form a composite picture of the Christian wife and mother who is temperate, pure in heart and life, devoted to her home, Christ-like, and dedicated to her husband. Again it should be noted that older women were to *teach* younger women to be this kind of person. This implies spiritual and emotional development. In other words, a woman does not suddenly become the perfect wife and mother. She must develop these characteristics.

FOR GROUP DISCUSSION AND INTERACTION

CASE STUDY

Jane could not tolerate success in her husband. She could never compliment him, either privately or publicly. In fact, when he did succeed in various activities, she would always find something critical to say.

It was also obvious that she was not a happy person. She did not enjoy her role as a wife or mother, nor did she find emotional or physical satisfaction in their sexual relationship.

1. Have you ever met a woman like Jane?
2. What seems to be her problem or problems?

ADDITIONAL QUESTIONS

1. What practical steps can a Christian wife take who is married to a man who does not take the leadership in the home? How can she handle this delicate situation?
2. What can a wife do to help her husband who is not achieving his vocational goals? How can she assist him without threatening him still further?

5

CHILDREN—THEIR PLACE IN
GOD'S PLAN

CHAPTERS 18 and 19 of Matthew's gospel record three significant statements Jesus made about children. Profound in meaning, each could serve as a sermon text.

Do not offend them. On one occasion Jesus used a child to teach His disciples the true meaning of humility. While discussing the characteristics of child life, He warned against offending children. "If anyone leads into sin one of these little ones who believe in Me, it would be better for him to have a big millstone hung around his neck and be drowned in the lake where it's deep" (Mt 18:6, Beck[1]).

What a warning! To Jesus Christ, it was a terrible sin to lead a child astray. How important it is for parents to set a proper example for their children and to lead them in the way of righteousness.

Do not despise them. A little further along in this same chapter, Jesus gives another warning regarding adult attitudes toward children. Williams translates this imperative by saying, "Be careful not to look with scorn on a

1. *The New Testament in the Language of Today,* by William F. Beck.

single one of these little children" (v. 10).[2] In context, Jesus was talking about the importance of every child in the sight of God. He follows this statement with the potent illustration of the lost sheep and then drives home the application by saying, "Even so it is not the will of your Father which is in heaven, that one of these little ones should perish" (v. 14, KJV). How important it is for parents to promote the spiritual welfare of their own children and to lead them to a personal salvation experience!

Do not forbid them to come to Me. In chapter 19 Jesus demonstrates what He has just taught. His disciples rebuked those who brought little children to Him (v. 13), as if Christ did not have time to waste on insignificant little ones. But Jesus said, "Let the little children alone, and stop preventing them from coming to me, for to such as these the kingdom of heaven belongs" (Mt 19:14, Williams).

Jesus Christ's attitude toward children leaves no doubt regarding their place in the plan of God. The totality of the written Word of God says more about children—their nature, their training, their problems—than any other subject related to the Christian home. This too speaks of the importance of child life.

A. Blessings from God

Children are a *blessing* from the Lord. The psalmist said, "As arrows are in the hand of a mighty man; so are children of the youth. Happy is the man that hath his quiver full of them" (Ps 127:4-5).

Again and again Scriptures speak of the blessing of having children, especially when they become "wise" children and walk in the ways of God (Pr 10:1; 15:20; 23:15,

2. *The New Testament—A Translation in the Language of the People,* by Charles B. Williams.

24, 25). The Word of God proclaims that "children's children are the crown of old men" (Pr 17:6). Not only are they a blessing to their parents, but nothing is more delightful to the heart of grandparents than to experience the blessing of having grandchildren.

One of the promises to the children of Israel before they entered the promised land was that God would bless them by giving them many children (Deu 7:13; Ps 128:3-4). The condition was that they were to hearken to the Word of God and obey His commandments. If they failed to "hearken unto the voice of the LORD thy God," they would be "cursed" rather than "blessed" (Deu 28:15, 18).

Since God dealt with Israel as a special nation, it would be unjust to conclude that parents today who are incapable of begetting children are suffering from God's judgment. However, Scripture is clear that children are truly a gift of God. All marriages so blessed have much for which to praise the Lord.

How different from the concept so frequently expressed in today's world! Children are often considered a burden rather than a blessing. There are reasons of course why it is sometimes advisable from a medical or psychological point of view to prevent the birth of children. But to plan a completely childless marriage for selfish, materialistic reasons has no scriptural support. This, it seems, is to miss out on one of God's richest blessings and to thwart the purpose and plan of God to "be fruitful, and multiply" (Gen 1:28).

B. Gifts from God

When Eve gave birth to her first son, Cain, she testified, "I have gotten a man from the LORD" (Gen 4:1). The miracle of birth is a gift of God. Every child born into this world is a testimony of His marvelous handiwork.

For years man has wondered at the phenomena of conception, of prenatal development, of the mechanism of heredity, and of birth itself. Maturation—the process of bring the various parts of the human organism to full development—reflects God's marvelous plan every time it takes place. From a one-celled being when new life begins, only 2/100 inch in diameter, the newborn has already developed into a complex being of more than 200 billion cells at birth.

And then there is postnatal development—almost a breath-taking process. That little newborn, so immature, so dependent, barely able to move, unable to see—soon becomes an active, growing bundle of energy.

Motor skills come first—grasping, crawling, pulling himself up. And then the capacity to learn! The little mass of cells known as the human brain begins to mature and to cry out for knowledge. Before the child can speak, he can understand. Before he can read, he can talk. By the time he is four, he has mastered fifteen hundred words. And this is the beginning of a vocabulary that soon reaches several thousand words.

Is this a product of chance, the result of a process of biological evolution? Impossible! The discoveries of science itself testify to the "miracle of procreation." Every time new life comes into being, it is a reflection of that original creation in the Garden, when God "formed man of the dust of the ground, and breathed into his nostrils the breath of life; and man became a living soul" (Gen 2:7).

Truly "children are an heritage of the LORD: and the fruit of the womb is his reward" (Ps 127:3). Even with his lack of laboratory knowledge so abundant today regarding human growth and development, David captured the spirit of wonderment that surrounds new life. "Thou hast covered me in my mother's womb," he said. "I will praise thee; for I am fearfully and wonderfully made" (Ps 139:13-14).

C. Gifts to God

Several well-known people in the Bible received children in direct answer to prayer (Gen 15:2; 25:21; Lk 1:13). One outstanding example is Hannah, who prayed earnestly for a son. She promised the Lord that if He gave her a child, she would "give him unto the LORD all the days of his life" (1 Sa 1:10-11).

God heard Hannah's request and gave her a son whom she named Samuel. Hannah conscientiously kept her promise and "lent" or more literally, "gave him to the LORD" (1:28) so that he might serve in the place of worship at Shiloh.

For Hannah, it was a great sacrifice to give up the son for whom she had prayed so earnestly. Any mother can imagine the emotional trauma that must have gripped her heart when she said good-bye to her little son, who was probably only three years old at the time. But God rewarded Hannah for her faithfulness. He gave her not only more sons but daughters also (2:21).

It should be noted that Elkanah, Hannah's husband, was in complete sympathy with Hannah's desire. Throughout the text, it is obvious he was just as concerned as she that they have a son. And he was also willing to give him to the Lord. He wished only that God's will be done (1:23).

Though the literal events in this story are not intended to be reproduced in the Christian home today, there is an important principle which applies to every Christian father and mother. Since children are a gift from God, can parents do less than dedicate them to the Lord for whatever purpose He has planned? Just as every Christian is not his own (1 Co 6:19), so children do not really belong to parents. They are theirs to love, to train, to enjoy. But God wants every child born into a Christian home as His very own, to use as He desires. Thus, in the spirit of Hannah and Elkanah, children should be dedicated to the Lord before they are born. Many churches provide opportunity for public dedication of children which is a commendable plan and truly a lovely and solemn occasion.

FOR GROUP DISCUSSION AND INTERACTION

1. In view of Jesus Christ's attitude toward children, what implications can be drawn and what guidelines set up for the Christian education of children both in the home and the church?
2. In view of the increased problems in rearing a large family in our society, what is a practical but scriptural approach to this issue?

6

BIBLICAL CHILD PSYCHOLOGY

A. Jesus as a Child

JESUS GREW as any normal person. Like a true physician, Dr. Luke delineated four specific areas of human growth and development: "And Jesus increased in wisdom and stature, and in favour with God and man" (Lk 2:52).

First, *Jesus increased in wisdom—mental growth.* How the omniscient Creator could voluntarily restrict His knowledge and develop intellectually is beyond our ability to comprehend. Yet he did.

Second, *Jesus increased in stature—physical growth.* The invisible God took upon Himself the form of man. Though conceived by God the Spirit in the virgin Mary, He had a normal human birth. He manifested all the natural maturational patterns of childhood and adolescence.

Third, *Jesus increased in favor with God—spiritual growth.* Even more difficult to understand is the development of our Lord's human spirit. As the only perfect human since Adam's fall, He "grew, and waxed strong in spirit" and "the grace of God was upon him" (2:40).

Fourth, *Jesus increased in favor with man—social growth.*

This statement in context reveals that Jesus had just amazed the doctors in the temple with His wisdom and knowledge (vv. 46-47). Jesus grew in relationship to people around Him. His personality showing through His humanity was gracious.

It is interesting to note that psychologists today frequently speak of a child's personality in terms of mental, physical, spiritual and social development. Here, hundreds of years before a scientific study of children revealed their growth patterns, the Word of God set forth a divine pattern. And of no little significance, this divine pattern was used of the Son of God, who was true and perfect man as well as true and undiminished God.

B. Children Are Children

In 1 Corinthians 13—the great love chapter of the Bible—Paul draws upon the experience of child life to illustrate spiritual immaturity. In the process he states an important idea—that children are children (v. 11).

First, *a child speaks as a child,* not as a young person or an adult. He has his own limited vocabulary, depending on his age and his opportunities for learning. He verbalizes out of a limited background of experience, not having the depth of insight that older people have. He thinks and speaks what he feels at the moment, regardless of circumstances or environment.

Second, *a child understands* or, more appropriately, *thinks like a child.* What the child says is actually a reflection of what he thinks and the way he thinks. His limitations in thinking result not only from lack of experience but also because his brain has not fully developed. Medical science states that the average person's brain does not fully mature biologically until the teen years.

Third, *a child reasons or plans like a child.* Closely related to *thinking*, this characteristic seems to involve the inability to utilize knowledge in a profitable way. He is unable to integrate his knowledge as a mature individual does. Perhaps this refers to the child's lack of wisdom.

Frequently adults become impatient with children's behavior. We often think of them as "little men and women," not as "little people." They will be children until they mature sufficiently in all facets of their personalities and become "adults." Parents constantly need to remind themselves of this truth. Pushing a child beyond his ability and demanding more from him than he is capable of producing has often created problems in all facets of a child's personality—physical, mental, social and spiritual.

One of the most common problems is that the child becomes hostile and resentful, developing deep feelings of anxiety and guilt. Sometimes these experiences cause the child to have unconscious feelings of hostility toward parents which last into the teen years and even into adulthood (see Eph 6:4).

C. In the Way He Should Go

"Train up a child in the way he should go: and when he is old, he will not depart from it" (Pr 22:6).

This verse is probably one of the most quoted verses from the Old Testament, particularly in relation to child training. The primary meaning of *train up* is to put something in the mouth. Out of this grew the idea of restraining a horse with a bit, and then dedicating a temple or house. The postbiblical meaning of the word is "to catechize" and "to educate."

Both the Old and New Testaments use a variety of words to refer to child training, such as "to teach," "to chasten, discipline or correct," "to guide or direct," and "to reprove." There is abundant evidence that the Holy Spirit was vitally concerned that children be brought up "in the nurture and admonition of the Lord" (Eph 6:4).

Interestingly, the phrase "in the way he should go" is another illustration of psychological truth that was in the Word of God long before it grew out of scientific study. This verse refers to "the child's way," to the "nature of the child as such." In other words, the Word of God implies that the instruction of children should be related to their nature and carried out according to the various stages of life.

Practically speaking, this means that both what is taught and the way it is taught should be determined by the child's mental, physical, social and spiritual characteristics. He cannot be expected to perceive and understand truth that is beyond his ability to grasp. He should not be forced to learn in circumstances that will go contrary to his normal physical and psychological patterns of development, for this will result in frustration, distraction, pent-up emotions, and even hostility.

Christian parents, therefore, should carefully evaluate the methods and techniques they are using to train their children. To follow correct psychological and educational principles is important in determining whether or not a child will develop into a well-balanced and adjusted Christian personality.

D. "Line Upon Line"

A passage of Scripture closely related to Proverbs 22:6 is Isaiah 28:9-10. In some respects its teachings represent the other side of the educational coin. The verses in Proverbs seem to refer to the nature of the child, whereas Isaiah speaks of content or doctrine. Both are linked closely together, however, by appropriate methods of training.

The order in which the various educational elements appear in these verses is significant. First, *there is content.* "Whom shall he teach knowledge? and whom shall he make to understand doctrine?" (v. 9). The Word of God, of course, is the most important content for child training in the home. It must be central, not peripheral. From the Scriptures come the objectives and goals to be reached in the life of each child—to bring to Christ, to build up in Christ, to send out for Christ. And from the Scriptures also come the truth and knowledge to achieve these objectives.

Second, *there is the child himself.* "Them that are weaned from the milk, and drawn from the breasts." This, of course, implies that training must begin early. The previous lesson teaches that this training process must be according to the nature of the child and carried out in conjunction with his various stages of life.

Third, *there is methodology.* This is the link between the Word of God and the child in the process of teaching. There must be *continuity* in teaching—"precept upon precept" and "line upon line" (v. 10). As the late Dr. Henrietta Mears said, "The Bible includes milk for babies, bread for youth, and meat for men." When teaching children in the home, parents must utilize Bible content carefully according to the age level of the child and teach it in an orderly manner. Fortunately, there are many good books today to assist parents in doing this.

But there must also be *appropriateness in amount*—"here a little, and there a little." Again, this is determined by age level, attention span, and interest.

FOR GROUP DISCUSSION AND INTERACTION

Various studies seem to indicate that the oldest child frequently develops more of a perfectionist personality than the children who come along later. Consequently, he shows more anxiety about failure to measure up to certain standards he has set for himself. He may take life so seriously that it interferes with natural childhood experiences in growth and development.

1. Why do you suppose this happens?
2. What suggestions can be given to help young couples overcome this problem with their first child?

GROUP PROJECT

Divide into several groups and discuss the fourfold needs of children at various age levels. The following chart will clarify this project:

Areas of Growth and Development		Mentally	Physically	Spiritually	Socially
Ages	0-1				
	2-3				
	4-5				
	6-8				
	9-11				

7

BIBLICAL PEDAGOGY

A. More Than Family Worship

WHILE ISRAEL was in the plains of Moab, just prior to their entrance into the promised land, Moses gave them parting instructions. In two key passages, he emphasized the importance of continuing to instruct children in the Word of God (Deu 6:6-9; 11:18-21).

First, Moses warned that the truth he was imparting to them was to be in their own hearts and souls (6:6; 11:18). Parents cannot effectively teach something which is not a deep and abiding conviction of their own.

Second, Moses said of the words of God, "Thou shalt teach them diligently unto thy children" (6:7). He then proceeded to tell where and when the Word was to be taught—when sitting in the house, when walking, when retiring in the evening, when arising in the morning. In other words, teach everywhere and at all times.

Not only were they to talk about the commands of the Lord, but, said Moses, "Thou shalt bind them for a sign upon thine hand, and they shall be as frontlets between thine eyes. And thou shalt write them upon the posts of thy house, and on thy gates" (vv. 8-9). Whether this language was to be figurative or literal, the meaning is clear. The Word of God was to be kept before the eyes of the younger members of the family to cause their children to both *hear* and *see* the Word of God.

Frequently in the Christian home today, parents feel they have performed their duty when they have conducted a family worship period, including Bible instruction and prayer. A regular time for family worship each day is commendable and is to be encouraged, but the Word of God clearly teaches this is not enough. The total atmosphere of the home is to be saturated with the presence of God. Christian training is not to be relegated to a "period," but is to be constant, natural, and meaningful. One of the most significant ways to create this type of learning situation is by parental example. When a child "sees" as well as "hears" the Word of God, profound impressions are made on his life. But when he "hears" and does not "see" the reality of Christ in his parents' lives, he becomes confused and disillusioned, and often begins to doubt the Bible.

In my family, some of the greatest teaching and worship experiences over the years have been spontaneous and unplanned—while walking through the woods, around a campfire on a secluded beach, when driving along in the car, at night as each child is tucked into bed, in the middle of a meal or—believe it or not—even in the middle of a family TV special.

Look for these opportunities. They are there and provide opportunities to plug into a child's life at the reality level.[1]

1. For an excellent sound colored film presenting this concept, see the film, *The Christian Home: Problems and Priorities*, featuring Dr. Howard G. Hendricks, available from: Space Age Communications—Educational, Box 11008, Dallas, Texas 75223.

B. The Mother and Child Training

The Scriptures give several illustrations of a mother's love, concern, and care for her child. For example, Moses' mother hid him in the bulrushes to save his life (Ex 2:1-10). Hannah visited Samuel once a year to bring him a coat (1 Sa 2:19). Isaiah reminds us that it is rare for a mother to forget her baby (Is 49:15).

Paul says of himself and his co-workers, "We proved to be gentle among you, as a nursing mother tenderly cares for her own children (1 Th 2:7, NASB).

When a baby is born, the mother is the most important person in his life. Humanly speaking, he is totally dependent on her for all his needs. Because of this close contact, it is she whom he first recognizes. He becomes aware of his mother before he becomes aware of himself.

Clinical psychologists remind us regularly from their everyday experiences in working with people who have emotional and mental difficulties, that the mother's influence on her children is very important. Basic feelings of security or insecurity, acceptance or rejection, love or hate, are often formed in the very early years of a child's life. Educational psychologists remind us that these basic emotional patterns are also significant in affecting the way a child learns or does not learn. Thus a mother, even before verbal communication can take place, is communicating with her child and preparing him for the time when he can appropriate instruction on a rational level.

The Christian mother in a home where the father is not saved is in an even more strategic position. Perhaps Timothy's mother, Eunice, is an illustration of this, for the Scripture says that she "was a Jewess, and believed," but her husband "was a Greek" (Ac 16:1). If so, she is an excellent example, for she taught Timothy from the time he was very small (2 Ti 3:15) and helped to instill in his heart a deep and abiding faith in God. This faith became the basis of Timothy's personal commitment to Christ and of his extensive ministry. What great influence the mother has upon her child! What a contribution she can make to the cause of Christ!

C. The Father and Child Training

Fathers *are to bring up their children* "in the nurture and admonition of the Lord" (Eph 6:4). God said of Abraham, "I know him, that he will command his children and his household after him, and they shall keep the way of the LORD, to do justice and judgment" (Gen 18:19). Though the mother is responsible for the early nurture of the child, the Bible clearly teaches that fathers are directly responsible for teaching their children the Word of God.

Fathers are not to provoke their "children to anger, lest they be discouraged (Col 3:21). A Christian father, whether he recognizes it or not, influences his children in unusual ways. As the God-appointed leader in the home, he must be careful not to use his authority as an excuse to vent his own pent-up emotions, to display his own feelings of frustration.

Paul states that it is possible through improper discipline to "discourage children," to thwart their motivation, to create emotional difficulties. This truth is perhaps more profound than we like to admit. The fact of the matter is that children, consciously and unconsciously, often identify their heavenly Father with their earthly father. If their earthly father is unloving, unkind, unfair, thus creating fear, hostility, and other negative emotions, a child will frequently transfer his mental images and emotional feelings to God. Christian psychologists who work closely with Christian youth who are suffering from emotional problems, discover that an inability to relate properly to

God through faith and prayer often is caused by deep feelings of hostility toward a father or mother. Some youth who have difficulty feeling "accepted by God," who have doubts regarding their salvation, may never have felt accepted by their parents.

I shall never forget overhearing one of my own daughters talking with her sister one day and explaining that God was her "heavenly Daddy." It was a rather jolting experience to be reminded so vividly that her image of her heavenly Father and her feelings about Him were a reflection of how she viewed her earthly father. A sobering thought, indeed!

D. The Individual Touch

Our motives were pure, and we were utterly honest," said Paul to the Thessalonian Christians. "We treated you like a nursing mother tenderly cares for her children, and loved you so dearly we were willing to have died for you. We worked night and day, lived holy lives, and just like a father teaches his own children one by one, we ministered to you" (author's paraphrase of 1 Th 2:1-11).

Twice in this passage, Paul draws upon the family unit to illustrate his and his coworkers' ministry when they founded the church in Thessalonica (Ac 17:1-9). The first reference is to the mother (1 Th 2:7), as mentioned in a previous section. The second illustrates Paul's vision of a true Christian father (2:11).

Paul believed in the "individual touch." Arthur Way captures the full intent of verse 11 when he translates: "You know, how with each of you, *one by one*, as a father with his own children, I pleaded, how I encouraged you, how I adjured you."[2]

2. Arthur S. Way, *The Letters of St. Paul*, 8th ed. (Chicago: Moody, 1950), pp. 5-6. Itals. added.

One great mistake in many Christian families is that parents just rear a family rather than individuals in the family. Children are all different, even though closely knit in a family unit. Each has a distinct personality, separate needs, varied interests. Some of these differences are caused by heredity, others by environment. Each child needs to be treated as an individual.

This is not to advocate partiality or unfairness. Rather, it means giving each child his own personal and private share of attention. It means spending time with each one, getting to know each one, and encouraging each one. It means listening to each child's individual problems, sharing in the happiness and joy of each one's interests, and meeting each one's personal needs, both spiritually and psychologically.

If Paul considered this approach important in working with Christians generally, how important it is in the home! We must remember that Jesus Christ set the supreme example in practicing the "individual touch," as illustrated in His relationship with His disciples, Nicodemus, the woman at the well, the blind man, and many others. He dealt with them one by one.

E. Parental Consistency

Of all subjects related to child training, none is more important than parental consistency. The Scriptures not only state emphatically that those who sin will reap what they sow (Gal 6:7), but show that a parent cannot sin without affecting his children. In Numbers 14:18 we read: "The LORD is longsuffering, and of great mercy, forgiving iniquity and transgression, and by no means clearing the guilty, visiting the iniquity of the fathers upon the children unto the third and fourth generation." (See also Ex 20:4-5.)

"How can this be?" many ask. Medical and psychological information help us grasp one significant aspect of this scriptural statement. In the most part, it *does not* seem to mean that there will be some hereditary carry-over from one generation to another. Rather, this truth seems to be related to the environment that is usually created for years to come and the psychological and spiritual effects which result.

Perhaps this can best be explained by a true but unidentifiable example. Suppose a "Christian" father and mother live a very inconsistent life. There is no real love between the parents, although the family is large. There is constant fighting, bickering, and no concern whatsoever for the spiritual welfare of the children. Yet the parents attempt to portray before outsiders that they are spiritual. As a result, several of the children grow up to deny the faith altogether. Others become so frustrated attempting to live the Christian life that they give up in despair.

How many generations may need to pass before the effects of this sin will no longer be evident? The fact is that three, four, even five generations of children may be affected, and it is conceivable that the descendants of those who denied the faith may never become Christian.

Make no mistake about it, sin leaves its mark. Because David broke the law of God in committing adultery and murder, God said that the sword would never depart from his house (2 Sa 12:10-11), even though he was completely forgiven of his sins. The sins of David's own children created his deepest grief (2 Sa 13:1-22; 15; 1 Ki 1:5).

How solemn is God's warning to all Christian parents! But also how glorious is the promise for those who truly walk in the Spirit (Gal 6:7-9)!

FOR GROUP DISCUSSION AND INTERACTION

A Christian high school girl was deeply troubled about her

relationship with her parents and the Lord. She felt that God was displeased with her no matter how hard she tried through spiritual exercises (prayer and Bible study). She never felt completely accepted by God. Actually the root of the problem centered in her relationship with her parents with whom she never felt complete acceptance. No matter how hard she had tried she had never been able to please them, especially her father. Consequently she had transferred these feelings to her heavenly Father. God had become another authority figure in her life—One whom she tried hard to please, but who never fully accepted her.

1. Why is this problem even more severe when the parents are Christians?
2. What specific suggestions can be given to help this girl overcome her problem?
3. How can this problem be prevented in a Christian home?
4. Why does this problem happen in a Christian home?

8

BIBLICAL OBJECTIVES

How OLD must a child be before Christian training should begin? Paul said of Timothy, "From a child thou hast known the holy scriptures" (2 Ti 3:15). The word "child" in this verse refers to a very small baby.

How can a child this small be made aware of the Word of God? When thinking of Bible instruction, we naturally think of "words" and the use of sound symbols to convey concepts and ideas. But must parents wait until their children can understand and use words before they communicate the Word of God to them?

Not at all! If they wait until their children can comprehend propositional truth as it is communicated verbally, they have already waited too long. By the time a child has acquired a vocabulary of just two hundred to three hundred words, he is already three years old. Parents dare not wait until then to begin teaching him.

Long before a child can say "daddy" or "mommy," he can "read"—not words, of course, but parents' lives. Long before he can comprehend the Bible words, "Children, obey your parents," he can hear and comprehend certain sounds. Though these sounds may be unintelligible to him as far as verbal comprehension is concerned, he soon learns to associate meaning with these sounds. The meaning he associates with verbal and visual expression is the way he interprets the spirit in which a person speaks or acts. It is not necessary for him to understand or use words to be able to interpret the concepts of love-hate, gladness-sadness, kindness-bitterness, selfishness-unselfishness, friendliness-unfriendliness.

How old must a child be before parents begin to teach him the Word of God? They must start as soon as he is born, for this is when he begins to observe, to feel and to interpret expressions. Psychologists tell us that by the time a child is two (when the average child is just beginning to use words), many of his basic personality traits and habit patterns are already molded. The attitudes he has observed in his parents regarding God, Jesus, the Bible, and other members of the family have already influenced his own personality development.

A. Wise Unto Salvation

What is the primary purpose of early training in the home? The apostle answers this question when he says to Timothy, "From a child thou hast known the holy scriptures, which are able to make thee wise unto salvation through faith which is in Christ Jesus" (2 Ti 3:15).

Children need to be converted. Every child even though he may be publicly dedicated or baptized, needs to recognize that he is a sinner in need of forgiveness and consequently receive Jesus Christ as personal Saviour. A view of Christian nurture that does not include this very important decision is not based on the Word of God. The Bible clearly teaches that to be saved, one must personally receive Christ as an act of the will (Jn 1:12; Ac 16:31). A father's or mother's faith, or any special act by them or by the preacher, will not save the children (Jn 1:13). Parents are responsible, therefore, to lead their children to Christ when they are old enough to understand conversion, at least in its simplest meaning.

Children are converted at various ages. The age of conversion varies greatly. Some children receive Christ at a very early age—even at three or four years. The most common age ranges between six and eleven, during the primary and junior years.

No child "can say that Jesus is the Lord, but by the Holy Ghost" (1 Co 12:3). True conversion is a result of the Holy Spirit's work in the heart (Jn 16:8-11). Parents should be alert to that time when the Spirit is at work in the heart of a child enlightening and convicting of sin.

Unsaved children do not necessarily live in open rebellion against God. Parents should never take for granted that their children are saved because they pray, show an interest in spiritual things, and are generally "good." If children are properly trained from early childhood, they do not ordinarily become "great sinners." But they are sinners nevertheless (Ro 3:23). The transition "out of darkness into light" may be a very quiet and unemotional experience; but if sincerely made, the decision is just as real and meaningful as that made by one who has lived many years in the ways of the world.

B. Instruction in Righteousness

After a child or young person in the home receives Jesus Christ as personal Saviour, it is important that he be instructed in the Word of God. As a newborn babe, he needs to learn to "desire the sincere milk of the word," that he "may grow thereby" (1 Pe 2:2).

After writing to Timothy and reminding him of his own experiences with the Word of God from early childhood which made him "wise unto salvation" (2 Ti 3:15), Paul goes on to state that the Scriptures are also useful and necessary for growth in the Christian life and for instruction in righteous living (v. 16).

All Scripture is profitable for doctrine; that is, for teaching. There is no greater source of knowledge than the Scriptures. Every child should be taught the Word of God in the home by precept and example. Whatever else is taught should be secondary to the Word of God.

All Scripture is profitable for reproof. The noun here rendered "reproof" is related to the verb "reprove" in John 16:8. Using the Word of God, the Holy Spirit causes personal recognition of the truth. Every child, youth, and adult needs to be taught the Word of God, which serves to convince him of his sins and of the necessity of receiving Christ as his personal Saviour (Ro 10:17).

All Scripture is profitable for correction. Correction means "restoration" or "improvement." Again, no other knowledge is as powerful and effective as the Word of God in reforming man's behavior and in restoring him to right living. For those Christians who go astray, the Word of God will serve as a corrective means to bring them back on the right track.

All Scripture is profitable for instruction in righteousness. Children need not only be convinced of the truth of Christianity and to be restored and corrected, but they also need to be taught what is right and proper. The Word of God tells how to live a holy and dedicated life. "Instruction in righteousness" must be "on-going," even for parents. The challenge of the New Testament is to measure up to the stature of Christ (Eph 4:13).

C. Equipped to Serve

We have looked at two important objectives for the Christian home: (1) to lead each child to Christ at that moment when the Spirit of God enlightens his mind and convicts him of sin (2 Ti 3:15); and (2) to instruct each child in righteous and holy living (v. 16).

We come now to the ultimate goal, the result of the first two, *to equip each child to faithfully serve Jesus Christ.*

The New American Standard Bible translates 2 Timothy 3:17 "That the man of God may be adequate, equipped for every good work." Every Christian parent should attempt to reproduce himself in his own children—not in the sense of a life vocation but in terms of dedicated Christian living and service. The goal of every Christian home should be to produce a "man of God." As defined by Paul in 1 Timothy 6:11-12, a "man of God" is one who flees materialistic interests and follows after righteousness, godliness, faith, love, patience, meekness. He fights the good fight of faith and lays hold of eternal life.

Children who are taught well in the Word become men and women of God who are adequately prepared and equipped to work for Him. No matter what their specific vocations in life, they are called upon to be personal witnesses for Christ (Ac 1:8) and to become actively involved in the work of their church. They are to exercise their spiritual gifts in Christian service (Eph 4:11-12). If God should call them to serve as pastors or missionaries, they will be ready to go. If God should call them to serve as laymen working in some capacity in the church, they will be ready to work. The guiding principle for mature, well-equipped children of God is that they always want to know "what is that good, and acceptable, and perfect, will of God" (Ro 12:2).

D. The Rewards for Faithful Parents

The Bible speaks clearly of the rewards parents will experience if they faithfully train their children.

They will experience earthly joy and happiness. One of the greatest joys for Christian parents is seeing their children grow into adulthood and follow in the ways of God. "The father of the righteous shall greatly rejoice. . . . thy father and thy mother shall be glad" (Pr 23:24-25; see 10:1; 15:20). "The just man walketh in his integrity" and "his children are blessed after him" (20:7).

It is not difficult to discover living illustrations of the truth spoken in these verses. Wherever a Christian family has grown together in the Lord with common objectives and spiritual unity, there is joy and happiness, especially in the hearts of the parents. As they observe their grown children walking in spiritual paths, there is blessing and deep satisfaction.

They will also experience eternal rewards and blessing. Even more important than earthly rewards are heavenly rewards. When Paul spoke of his ministry among the Thessalonians, he wrote these significant words: "For what is our hope, or joy, or crown of rejoicing? Are not even ye in the presence of our Lord Jesus Christ at his coming? For ye are our glory and joy" (1 Th 2:19-20). Paul's motivation to minister to people came from two sources: first, his love for people, and second, the prospect of meeting these people in heaven.

Here is a spiritual lesson for all parents. What will make faithful parenthood worthwhile? Earthly joy in seeing children come to Christ and walk in His ways? Yes! But far more! The crowning joy and reward will be when parents and children rejoice together in that day when Christ comes to call all Christians home to glory. How wonderful it will be to hear His words, "Well done, thou good and faithful servant" (Mt 25:21). What rejoicing there will be when father, mother, sons and daughters together worship God in that day, saying, "Blessing, and glory, and wisdom, and thanksgiving, and honour, and power, and might, be unto our God forever and ever. Amen" (Rev 7:12).

FOR GROUP DISCUSSION AND INTERACTION

J. A. Hadfield, a secular psychologist, observes the following about teaching children moral values: "We see . . . that it is by a perfectly natural process that the child develops standards of behavior and a moral sense. So that if you never taught a child one single moral maxim, he would nevertheless develop moral—or immoral—standards of right and wrong by the process of identification."[1]

In another section he says: "What about *teaching* moral principles? Certainly the teaching of principles like generosity, kindness, industry, and perseverance is of great value, because such teaching transforms the subconscious process of identification into a conscious acceptance of abstract ideas and ideals, which can then be applied to all occasions. But remember that a child will accept only the teaching of one with whom he is identified, and will reject the teaching of one he dislikes."[2]

1. Assuming these are correct observations, what are the implications of these statements for Christian education in the home during the early years of a child's life?
2. How can Christian truth be taught apart from verbalizing it?

1. J. A. Hadfield, *Childhood and Adolescence* (Baltimore, Maryland: Penguin Books, 1967), p. 134.
2. *Ibid.*, p. 145.

9

CHRISTIAN DISCIPLINE

A. A Principle of Scripture

For consider Him who has endured such hostility by sinners against Himself, so that you may not grow weary and lose heart. You have not yet resisted to the point of shedding blood, in your striving against sin; and you have forgotten the exhortation which is addressed to you as sons, "My son, do not regard lightly the discipline of the LORD, nor faint when you are reproved by Him; for those whom the LORD loves He disciplines, and He scourges every son whom He receives." It is for discipline that you endure; God deals with you as with sons; for what son is there whom *his* father does not discipline? But if you are without discipline, of which all have become partakers, then you are illegitimate children and not sons. Furthermore, we had earthly fathers to discipline us, and we respected them; shall we not much rather be subject to the Father of spirits, and live? For they disciplined us for a short time as seemed best to them, but He disciplines us for our good, that we may share His holiness. All discipline for the moment seems not to be joyful, but sorrowful; yet to those who have been trained by it, afterwards it yields the peaceful fruit of righteousness (Heb 12:3-11, NASB).

The author of the book of Hebrews uses parental discipline to illustrate how God the Father frequently must deal with His spiritual children. He reminds us that chastening is a sign of God's love (12:6) and of our true relationship to Him (vv. 7-8) and a means to holy and righteous living (v. 11). Though difficult to endure, it is necessary for every child of God and in the end yields "the peaceable fruit of righteousness."

Discipline is therefore a principle of Scripture. It is necessary in the family of God and within every human family. The Bible knows nothing of the concept of total freedom so prevalent in today's world. Not to discipline children in the home is to violate the teachings and example of God.

The book of Proverbs contains a number of references which speak of discipline. Parents are to chasten their children "while there is hope" (19:18), use the rod of correction to drive foolishness from their hearts (22:15), correct them and deliver them from spiritual destruction (23:13-14), and discipline them in order to instill wisdom (29:15). Furthermore, Proverbs 29:17 says, "Correct thy son, and he shall give thee rest; yea, he shall give delight unto thy soul." But an undisciplined child will bring shame and disgrace to his parents (v. 15).

Anyone who believes the Bible cannot deny that discipline is necessary in the home. However, it must be administered for one basic purpose: to benefit the child. To use discipline as a means for displaying hostility or releasing tension, and to provoke one's children to wrath (see Eph 6:4) is sinful and disgraceful and will secure only bad results in the child. Discipline must be fair, just, and meted out in accordance with the wrong that has been done.

Anyone can "swing a rod," but only a truly dedicated Christian who has control of his own spirit knows when to do it, where to do it, and how. Discipline, therefore, is a solemn responsibility and must always be done in love.

Love and self-discipline are products of the Holy Spirit's control. The Spirit-disciplined believer is best qualified to provide discipline for his children.

B. Obedience and Honor

The Word of God not only instructs parents about their relationship to their children, but it also speaks to children about their relationship to their parents. In Ephesians Paul says, "Children, obey your parents in the Lord" (6:1); in Colossians he adds, "Children, obey your parents in all things" (\3:20).

The apostle gives two important reasons obedience to parents is necessary.

First, it is the right thing to do (Eph 6:1) and second, obedience is pleasing to the Lord (Col 3:20). To obey parents is to obey the Lord, for He has commanded it. In Proverbs God says that a child should "hear the instruction" of his father and "forsake not the law" of his mother (Pr 1:8; 6:20). One of the Ten Commandments reads: "Honour thy father and thy mother: that thy days may be long upon the land which the Lord thy God giveth thee" (Ex 20:12). This command was not applicable only to the children of Israel as they gained entrance to the promised land but also to all children who know and love the Lord. The words "honour thy father and thy mother" occur at least eight times in the Bible, twice in the Old Testament and six times in the New. Paul quotes this Old Testament reference in Ephesians 6:2-3 and applies it to the New Testament church. God is pleased when children obey their parents, and He promises them a spiritual blessing.

It should be noted, however, that obedience is not natural. Because every child is born with an Adamic nature, the urge to do wrong, to sin, and to disobey grows stronger as he grows older. Thus, it is important that children re-receive Christ at an early age and experience the presence and power of the Holy Spirit who can enable them to fulfill their roles as obedient children.

We must remember, however, that "children *are* children" (see p. 40). With the normal desire to be active, combined with a natural tendency to sin, a child may often find it difficult to conform to parental standards. It is at this point that parents must carefully blend love, understanding, spiritual counsel, and firmness to help the child over the rough spots of life.

It should also be noted that children, particularly in the first three years of life, pass through natural phases which can be easily interpreted as sin patterns. In reality, they are normal patterns and must be accepted as such. For example, the child of about one year loves to attract attention to himself. About the second year he becomes extremely curious and automatically explores everything—including himself—and enters a "self-will" phase when he begins to learn that he has some control over the world.

Many Christian parents, viewing various expressions of the child through their adult eyes and experiences, interpret these natural phases as a demonstration of the "old nature." Natural forms of "attention getting" are interpreted as the expression of "natural selfishness." Curiosity, particularly of a sexual nature, is interpreted as perversion or inappropriate sexual behavior. Expressions of self-will are categorized as the beginning of a self-centered life.

There is no doubt that the sin nature comes into play early in life. But studies have demonstrated that these childhood expressions during the first three years of life are natural phases that are essential for normal development. They must be treated accordingly. For example, to withhold attention from a child only *increases* the desire for attention. To bear down hard on exploration of sex as unnatural and perverted only draws attention to the sexual nature of the child and may create perversion. To try to break the will of a three-year-old by "beating it out of him" may create a "spineless" person or may drive his feelings inward, resulting in repressed feelings of hostility which will eventually reveal themselves in teenage or even adult rebellion. Some Christian parents then actually create the opposite results they are attempting to achieve.

Every Christian parent needs to pray for wisdom to rear his children according to their natural growth patterns, both physically and psychologically. This seems to be the true meaning of Proverbs 22:6 (see p. 41). There must be control, but not over-control. There must be discipline, but not over-discipline. There must be standards, but not so high that they frustrate the child and "provoke him to wrath" (Eph 6:4).

Again it should be emphasized that these balances are especially important during the first three years of life. These are primarily preverbal years and a period of development characterized by many innate and God-created phases, including the need for attention, exploration, and the development of self-confidence. Handled appropriately—with wisdom and patience—these phases pass as the child develops mature physical and psychological controls.

C. Disobedience and Dishonor

Just as blessing is promised to children who obey and honor their parents, so there are unpleasant results for those who disobey and dishonor their parents.

Disobedience and dishonor bring sorrow to children

themselves. Proverbs gives severe warnings to him who "curseth his father or his mother" (Pr 20:20) or who mocks and despises his parents (30:17). Note that these are probably grown children—not small children. Rather than long life, he is promised obscurity and severe judgment. To deliberately disrespect parents is to ask for heartache and trouble. For children to reject their parents is to reject their God, and the Word of God promises only deep regret and sorrow. Absalom, for example, had every opportunity for blessing and great prominence in the kingdom. But his rebellion against his father, David, and his own household resulted in death.

Disobedience and dishonor cause sorrow for parents. "A foolish son is a grief to his father, and bitterness to her that bare him" (Pr 17:25). The Word of God also describes him as "the calamity of his father" (19:13). "He that wasteth his father, and chaseth away his mother, is a son that causeth shame, and bringeth reproach" (19:26).

Many parents have experienced deep sorrow and despair because of children who have rebelled against the Lord and His Word. But it should be noted that in many instances this behavior has resulted from failure to fulfill the proper parental role. A careful study of the Scriptures indicates that most (not all) homes where sons and daughters have been exceedingly and continually rebellious and sinful reveal an inconsistency in following God's standards and laws. For example, Eli's sons went bad because he did not restrain them (1 Sa 3:13). David's children sinned against the Lord because of his own terrible sin (2 Sa 12:10). The son mentioned in Leviticus 24, who openly blasphemed the Lord, was the son of "an Israelitish woman, whose father was an Egyptian" (Lev 24:10). He was the product of a home where the parents, according to God's standard, were unequally yoked (Deu 7:3-4).

Aaron's evil sons are another example (Lev 10:1-2). It will be remembered from the accounts of the Exodus that Aaron had not always been the most spiritual father.

Christians can claim the promise that if they properly train their children, they will not depart from the pathway set before them (Pr 22:6). Furthermore, as will be explained later, the Bible sets forth the behavior of children in the home as a criterion for measuring a father's qualifications to be a church leader (1 Ti 3:4-5). These references imply that God-fearing children are products of a properly managed home.

Today numerous child guidance clinics across the land provide professional counseling for parents with problem children. Interestingly, the staffs for such clinics—usually composed of a psychiatrist, a psychologist and a social worker—have discovered that many psychological problems of a functional nature are directly related to a problem that exists between the parents and the child. Consequently, most clinics begin with an analysis of husband-wife and parent-child relationships to determine causes for the difficulty, which may be manifesting itself in jealous behavior, extreme hostility, emotional outbreaks, stealing, lying, low grades at school, inability to concentrate, and rebellion against home codes, school rules, etc. Once again modern science has discovered truth that has been in the Scriptures for many years.

D. The Testing Ground for Church Leadership

God's Word clearly teaches that the Christian home is a testing ground to determine whether a person is qualified to be a leader in the church.

In writing to Timothy, Paul says that one chosen to lead the church of God should be one who "ruleth well his own house" (1 Ti 3:4). He should have his children "in subjection with all gravity." They should respect and honor him because he is a serious-minded person, one who does not "provoke" them "to wrath" nor discourage them (Eph 6:4; Col 3:21).

In writing to Titus, the apostle adds that the one chosen to be a church leader should have "faithful children not accused of riot or unruly" (Titus 1:6). The word faithful is descriptive of those who are well-trained—those who are not accused of "riot" or of being "unruly," who have good character and are not given over to disorderly living.

Paul draws a specific comparison between the Christian family and the church of God. By asking a logical question, he brings the issue into clear focus: "For if a man know not how to rule his own house, how shall he take care of the church of God?" (1 Ti 3:5).

This is a graphic and beautiful illustration, for the church is also a "family," a fellowship of "brothers" and "sisters" in Christ who need guidance and direction from those who are God-appointed "shepherds." The qualities that make a good husband and father also make a good spiritual leader in the church. The abilities, skills, and Christian graces which develop God-fearing, respectful, and obedient children in the home also are used of God to develop mature, spiritual believers in the church.

How frequently this criterion is omitted in the average church when choosing a minister, an elder, a deacon. It is easy to deceive momentarily with a sparkling personality, a beautiful sermon, a happy disposition, or a serious approach to the world's problems. But there is one true test for a leader—one omitted so frequently! To know what kind of person the one under consideration for leadership really is, look carefully at his household.

E. Perilous Times

> This know also, that in the last days perilous times shall
> come. For men shall be lovers of their own selves, covet-
> ous, boasters, proud, blasphemers, disobedient to parents,
> unthankful, unholy, without natural affection, truce-
> breakers, false accusers, incontinent, fierce, despisers of
> those that are good, Traitors, heady, highminded, lovers
> of pleasures more than lovers of God; Having a form of
> godliness, but denying the power thereof: from such turn
> away (2 Ti 3:1-5).

Having emphasized the importance of parental example
and consistency it must also be remembered that the home
is not an isolated environment. Rather, it is part of a
larger community which in most instances is in contradiction to the standards of the Word of God. Therefore, to
establish a home solidly on Christian principles does not
guarantee that a child reared in that home will not come
in contact with sinful forces which may influence him to
depart from Christian standards.

We are privileged to live in a country that has been tra-
ditionally "Christian." For the most part our society has
functioned on the basis of the Protestant ethic—honesty,
integrity, and moral behavior in keeping with biblical
standards.

No longer is this true. In recent years, materialism,
secularism, atheism, and a changing moral climate have
catapulted the Christian home into a new and threatening
environment. No longer supported from without, the
Christian father and mother must face their task of Christian training as never before. It will take every ounce of
spiritual strength to combat the forces of Satan to keep the
home Christian, let alone make it an environment which
prepares children and youth "to stand against the wiles of
the devil" (Eph 6:11).

But not only are there forces which constantly bombard the Christian child and youth outside the home. Through modern technology, these influences are brought into the home by the flip of a switch or turn of a dial. Television commercials, carefully designed to motivate the deeper and more base emotions, are constantly viewed by Christian children. Unknown to parent or child, the subconscious is being tapped and set in motion toward ignoble actions.

Both radio and television blast forth "music" and visualize dancing that have deep psychological effects. While many Christian parents sit by and say, "It's a fad," many sociologists and psychologists who do not know our Lord vocalize the emotionally damaging effects of this new era in which we live.

Yes, the Christian home faces a challenge as never before! Are we prepared to meet this challenge?

FOR GROUP DISCUSSION AND INTERACTION

Bill was basically a "good" child most of his preteen life. Reared in a Christian home, he was obedient, quiet, submissive. In fact, people who visited in his home commented on his "good" behavior. He spent most of the time in his room, even as a small child, didn't "show off" in front of company, and when given the cue by his parents (a certain look) he said, "Yes, sir" and "No, ma'am" without hesitation.

His parents were proud of his behavior. When asked how they got such fantastic response, they proudly replied, "We began early!"

Now Bill is 18. He seldom comes home, resents his parents, has rejected Christianity, and never darkens the door of the church. In fact, he is thinking of dropping out of society.

His parents are heartbroken! When asked what happened, they reply, "We just don't know! We tried so hard!"

1. Could you give possible reasons for Bill's behavior?
2. What practical steps can be taken in a Christian home to keep this from happening?
3. Why is it easy for Christians to go to one extreme or another in disciplining their children?

10

DIVINE BALANCES AND FAMILY RESPONSIBILITIES

A. Divided Loyalties

SOME HAVE SUPPOSED that the apostle Paul was opposed to marriage. Nothing could be further from the truth (Eph 5:21-33). However, his tendency to be frank and realistic could, if taken out of context, lead some to wonder. But frankness and realism are needed in order to balance the unrealistic aura that youth, particularly, feel as they look forward to marriage.

In his first letter to the Corinthians Paul sets forth some of these realities. There shall be "trouble in the flesh" (1 Co 7:28), and one of the major tensions that may exist is *divided loyalties.* Paul points out clearly that those who are married have definite cares and responsibilities that make it necessary to give more time and effort to the marriage partner and less to direct service for the Lord (1 Co 7:32-33). He also makes it clear that this is true of both husband and wife.

Paul speaks first to the husband. "He that is married careth for the things that are of the world, how he may please his wife" (v. 33). This is normal, natural, and even a responsibility. But the temptation will come to lose that intricate balance that must exist between devotion to God and devotion to her. Herein lies the tension! He may spend more and more time attempting to please her and less and less time in prayer, Bible study and service for the Lord. He may find his affections growing stronger toward his wife, while his love for Christ diminishes. This calls for watchfulness.

Paul speaks next to the wife (v. 34). She, too, may be tempted to give more time and affection to her husband, while her relationship to Christ suffers. She may also be tempted to "adorn herself" in ways not becoming a Christian in order to gain greater attention from her husband.

What is the answer to this problem? First, couples must realize that this tension is normal. Second, they must seek to put Christ first in every relationship. Third, they must recognize with Paul, "I have been crucified with Christ; and it is no longer I who live, but Christ lives in me" (Gal 2:20, NASB). Fourth, they must let Christ live through them.

B. First Things First

God has given woman to man and man to woman in the marriage relationship because they need each other. They are to love each other dearly, respect each other's rights and needs, and seek each other's welfare.

God has also given children to bring blessing and happiness to the Christian home. Parents are responsible to love their children, to provide for them, to teach them, to discipline them—in short, to "bring them up in the nurture and admonition of the Lord" (Eph 6:4).

Children in turn are to love their parents, honor and obey them, and care for them in old age.

All these responsibilities and attitudes are biblical as we have seen from our study thus far. But these human relationships involving affection, loyalty, and dedication must be in proper perspective. It is clear that on the horizontal level—on the human plane—family members are to be first. But for the Christian family, there is a vertical relationship—man's love for God. This love must take precedence over love for husband or wife, father or mother, son or daughter (Mt 10:37). God *must* be first!

It is easy to become so involved in family life that God is given second place. Gifts for children, for husband or wife, for father and mother, can be given more prominence than gifts to God. Time spent in family pleasure can rule out time spent in the presence of the Lord. Plans for beautification of the home can rule out plans for serving the Saviour. Much activity in carrying out the routine of family living may keep us from the best.

Such was the case with Martha (Lk 10:38-42). When Jesus came to their home, her sister Mary chose to spend time with the Saviour. Martha was busy preparing for the Lord's visit. She became disturbed at Mary's behavior and made her feelings known. Jesus gently rebuked her and said, "One thing is needful: and Mary hath chosen that good part" (v. 42).

Martha's activity in the home was not wrong. She was fulfilling a responsibility, doing what was right and proper. But in her humanness she lost perspective. She needed to refocus her thinking. She had lost the divine balance, was putting her activity first. But *the Lord had to be first!*

C. Material Things Versus Materialism

After Moses had spoken so clearly to the children of Israel regarding their responsibility to teach their children (Deu 6:6-9), he gave a solemn warning about the subtle effects of materialism. "Beware," he said, "lest thou forget the LORD" (v. 12).

How easy it is to forget God when our houses are "full of all good things" and our wells are "digged," and our "vine-yards and olive trees" have provided us with food in abundance, and we have "eaten" and are "full" (v. 11). We become self-sufficient and say, "We did this ourselves." Then we become dissatisfied with enough and want more. Material blessings from God can easily lead to the sin of *materialism*.

One of the greatest threats to the Christian family in America is the impact of materialism. Never has there been so much for so few. And never have men forgot God as they are forgetting Him today.

God is being ruled out of the schools, out of the courts, and out of society as a whole. As wealth has increased, pleasures have increased. As salary scales have gone up, the work week has grown shorter. As conveniences have multiplied, so has boredom.

The Christian family is "in the world" and the greatest challenge it faces is not to become a part of the world (1 Jn 2:15). But members of a Christian home can be swept into the stream of materialism, and before they know what has happened their spiritual vision is blurred, their enthusiasm for evangelism and missions is dampened, and they no longer have time for the church. It is a known fact that youth who have grown up in our present "security-minded" environment are less interested in missionary service than those in previous years. The ministry interests them only as it provides a large salary and fringe benefits.

Make no mistake about it, materialism is having its effects on the Christian family! It is time for Christian parents to evaluate their motives, their interests, their concerns, and to remind themselves of the words of Jesus:

"Lay not up for yourselves treasures upon earth . . . but lay up for yourselves treasures in heaven" (Mt 6:19-20).

D. Responsibility for Parents

Jesus' rebuke of the Pharisees (Mk 7:9-13). To reveal their hypocrisy and sin, Jesus on one occasion referred to the Pharisees' attitude toward their parents. With great pride they claimed to keep the law of God, yet they had contrived a plan by which they could circumvent the fifth commandment, "Honour thy father and thy mother." They had established a tradition, a rule of their own, that a person might dedicate to God part of his wealth with the distinct purpose of being relieved of responsibility for his parents' welfare. By merely saying that his material goods were "corban," meaning dedicated to God for religious purposes, he then had no further responsibility for his parents.

Jesus condemned this practice as violating the law of God. The Pharisees were substituting the "commandments of men" for the "commandments of God." And of basic importance, their attitude was wrong. Their lack of real concern for their parents God recognized as a direct reflection of their lack of love for Him. "This people honoureth me with their lips, but their heart is far from me" (Mk 7:6), Jesus said, quoting Isaiah the prophet.

Jesus' example at the cross. Just before He died, Jesus demonstrated His concern when He asked John to care for His mother. Jesus probably died penniless, with nothing material to provide for His own. Yet He made provision for Mary's welfare. "Behold thy mother!" He said to John. "And from that hour that disciple took her unto his own home" (Jn 19:25-27). None could point a finger at Jesus and say He did not practice what He taught. What an example for all to follow!

Paul's word of admonition. The apostle Paul expressed concern that children provide for their parents who are in need when he said, "If any provide not for his own, and specially for those of his own house, he hath denied the faith, and is worse than an infidel" (1 Ti 5:8). He was speaking of children whose mother is widowed. The "first duty" of children and grandchildren, said Paul, is to "respect their own family and repay their parents, because that pleases God" (1 Ti 5:4, Beck).

E. Providing for Needy Family Members

Throughout the Bible, a number of references are made to God's concern for the "fatherless" and "widows." They seem to stand under His special guardianship and care. God said He would do justice to them (Deu 10:18) and preserve them (Jer 49:11). He also instructed His people not to afflict them (Ex 22:22) nor oppress them (Jer 7:6) nor take advantage of them (Deu 24:17). Rather, they were to feed (Deu 14:29), defend (Ps 82:3), and encourage them (Job 29:13). Isaiah said, "Learn to do well; seek judgment, relieve the oppressed, judge the fatherless, plead for the widow" (Is 1:17).

This obligation of God's people set forth so frequently in the Old Testament is reiterated in the New. James calls this care for the fatherless and widows "pure religion and undefiled before God" (Ja 1:27). There is no doubt that the church has a certain responsibility toward family members who are in need.

Paul spoke specifically about the care of widows when writing to Timothy. The church at Ephesus was to "honour widows that are widows indeed" (1 Ti 5:3). They were probably to do this by providing for their needs from public funds (v. 7). A "widow indeed" was one who had no children or other relatives on whom she could depend for support. If there were relatives, they, not the church, were responsible for her care (vv. 5, 8). A "widow indeed" was also to be a spiritual person (v. 5), an aged woman who had been married only once (v. 9), who had a good reputation and did good works (v. 10).

Though some of the instructions in this passage may not be applicable to the church in American society, the basic principles are. The church *does* have a responsibility to care for needy family members—specifically children whose parents have died or women who have lost their husbands. For the latter, there is to be discretion, however, for any woman so honored must be a spiritual Christian without an adequate source of income and one who will not take advantage of the privileges granted by the church (vv. 11-15).

Group Discussion and Interaction

Study carefully Deuteronomy 6:10-12; 8:11-17; and Judges 2:8-10.

The second generation in Israel had grown up in the land which their fathers had won. This generation had inherited from its parents possession and enjoyment. It had settled down in the life of abundance to which it was born.

How does this Old Testament illustration relate to the present generation of youth in America? Note particularly Deuteronomy 8:17 and Judges 2:10.

group projects

Divide into three groups and discuss the following balances which must be maintained in the Christian home:

Group 1—Divided loyalties

Group 2—First things first

Group 3—Material things vs. materialism

Determine practical steps for maintaining these balances in the Christian home.

11

BIBLICAL EXAMPLES AND SPECIAL LESSONS IN FAMILY LIVING

A. Family Jealousy

Shortly after sin entered the human race as a result of the fall, the Bible records a sad story of family jealousy (Gen 4:2-15). Cain was the first son born to Adam and Eve; Abel, the second. Cain became an agriculturist; Abel, a shepherd.

In time they both brought offerings to the Lord. Cain brought some of his produce, and Abel brought an animal from his flock. God looked with pleasure upon Abel's offering and accepted it, but He rejected Cain's.

The result was anger! Cain's countenance fell and he grew bitter. God warned him of this behavior and promised to accept a proper offering (Gen 4:7). But Cain's hostility toward God turned into jealousy and hostility toward his brother and led to Abel's murder.

As far as can be ascertained from the text, Cain had no human reasons for becoming jealous of his brother. There is no evidence that he was unfairly treated in the home.

Rather, his anger was directed toward God who had rejected him for his failure to bring a proper offering in faith (Heb 11:4). His hostility was then transferred to his innocent and favored brother.

In family relationships there seem to be two stimuli for creating jealousy, though both are closely related. One relates to unjust or unfair treatment by parents which sets the sin nature in motion. A second relates to sin on the part of the jealous child, apart from motivation from parents or a brother or sister. In the first case, parents should seek to avoid provoking jealousy. In the second, they should seek to understand why it occurs.

In Cain's case, he was the elder brother. Perhaps his younger brother had been a threat to his superior place in the home. Perhaps Cain was proud of his vocation, which no doubt demanded greater strength and endurance. To be rejected under these circumstances only aggravated his sin problem.

Whatever the case, Cain gave way to his sin nature. He was out of fellowship with God. Since that day, all brothers and sisters have had to face the problem of sin. Parents who are wise will do everything in their power to help their children rise above the sin and be filled with the Spirit.

B. A Family Test

The experience of Abraham and Isaac in Genesis 22 is one of the most severe family tests of all times. Here a promise and a command were in direct contradiction. God had told Abraham that in his seed all nations would be blessed (Gen 12:3). To fulfill the promise, God had performed a miracle in giving Isaac to Abraham and Sarah in their old age. Now God asked Abraham to sacrifice this promised son as a burnt offering.

To offer a beloved son would have been test enough.

But to offer a son who was a direct gift from God in response to a divine promise was humanly inconceivable.

But Abraham, with the eye of faith, could see beyond the horizontal, beyond the human predicament. Had not God been faithful before? Had not God commanded and then guided when he had left his country and "went out, not knowing whither he went" (Heb 11:8)? Had not God directed when Abraham, by faith, "sojourned in the land of promise" as a stranger (v. 9)? Had not God performed a miracle when He gave Sarah "strength to conceive" (v. 11)? Abraham knew he could trust God again.

In God's sight, Abraham "offered up Isaac," for Abraham had no reservations. Questions? Yes, for he was human. But he did not argue with God. He proceeded in full faith, even trusting God for resurrection (v. 19).

After God had provided the ram, He again spoke to Abraham: "In thy seed shall all the nations of the earth be blessed; because thou hast obeyed my voice" (Gen 22:18).

God tested Abraham for a purpose—to prove his faith, his love, his willingness to obey. God sometimes tests the Christian family for the same purpose (1 Pe 1:7-8). Sickness, financial setbacks, frustration, stress, suffering, and death are a part of the Christian life. But nothing touches God's own but that His purposes are being fulfilled. When these inevitable trials knock at the door, we would do well to remember faithful Abraham (Gal 3:9) and many others who are "a cloud of witnesses" (Heb 12:1).

C. An Example of Family Forgiveness

One of the most interesting family stories recorded in the Bible revolves around Joseph, the son of Jacob (Gen 37-45). Because Joseph was born to him in his old age, Jacob developed an unusual love for him and did not hesitate to show it in the presence of his other sons. This family favoritism soon created bitter jealousy in the hearts of his brothers, and every move Joseph made seemed to create greater hatred toward him. Three times in Genesis 37 the words "they hated him" appear (vv. 4, 5, 8).

The events that followed are well known. When Joseph went to where his brothers were feeding their flocks in order to determine for his father if they were well, they "conspired against him to slay him" (v. 18). They eventually sold him to a caravan of Ishmaelites who in turn sold him to Potiphar, an officer of Egypt's Pharaoh.

Years of alternating adversity and exaltation followed for Joseph. Temptations, trials, false accusations and imprisonment eventuated in his promotion to second ruler of the kingdom (41:40). He exchanged a prison for a palace when he was able to interpret Pharaoh's dream.

The dream had to do with a great famine that was coming upon the land after a period of great plenty. Joseph became responsible to prepare for the hardships to come, which he did by building up a great surplus of food.

When the seven lean years occurred as Joseph had predicted, his own family was not exempt. Among those who came to Egypt to buy food from Joseph's great storehouses were his brothers (42:3). What an opportunity for revenge! He who had been so mistreated now was in control. Joseph's power was nearly as great as Pharaoh's. His chances for getting even were many—withholding food, imprisonment, or death.

Though Joseph disguised himself from his brothers and tested them, in his heart he could hold no grudge (v. 24). He completely forgave them and, after revealing himself to them, asked them to bring his aged father to Egypt along with their own households (45:1-13). Furthermore, he said, "I will give you the good of the land of Egypt, and ye shall eat the fat of the land" (v. 18). This was complete forgiveness!

No one would justify Jacob's sin in showing favoritism to Joseph or his brothers' evil treatment in hating him and selling him into Egypt. All this was wrong in God's sight and worthy of judgment.

Actually, an important lesson is to be learned from this family experience. Favoritism toward any one child creates difficulties and problems not only for the other children, but also for the parents and the one given special favors. That all of Joseph's brothers were suffering from the same hostile feelings toward him, reveals that Jacob had not even taken precautions to hide his greater love for Joseph. Their hatred was directed not only at Joseph but at Jacob too. To sell Joseph into Egypt was a way of getting even with their brother and with their father who had treated them unequally.

But in the midst of this family dissension, and later as he experienced misunderstanding and mistreatment in Egypt, Joseph learned an important secret. No matter what evil may come into his life, he discovered that his love for God and his loyalty to his sovereign Master were most important. He learned by direct experience that God can make "all things work together for good to them that love God, to them who are the called according to his purpose" (Ro 8:28).

When Jacob died, Joseph's brothers were still concerned about his attitude toward them. Evidently they could not fathom how Joseph could have so readily forgiven them. This, incidentally, is an outward sign of how deeply they hated him. They began to wonder if he had treated them well for their father's sake. But Joseph confirmed his true spirit of forgiveness when he said, "Fear not: for am I in the place of God? But as for you, ye thought evil against me; but God meant it unto good" (Gen 50:19-20).

His secret? God is sovereign in the life of a true believer and He permits nothing but what will ultimately benefit His child. Present trials and perplexing problems bring ultimate blessing and reward. If we recognize this truth and commit ourselves to the righteous Ruler, His peace will guide and guard us in our personal relationships.

D. The Son That Was Lost and Found

While Jesus was teaching one day, a group of publicans and sinners drew near to hear him. The Pharisees and scribes immediately criticized Him for welcoming these people and for eating with them (Lk 15:1-2). Perceiving their jealousy and unjust feelings, Jesus spoke several parables to reveal their error.

One of the stories was about a son who came to his father one day and asked for his own share of the family funds. He then left home and spent all that he had in wild and sinful living. With things going from bad to worse, he eventually found himself feeding swine in the fields in order to keep body and soul together.

Being in great need, and even wanting to eat what he was feeding the pigs, this son was gradually jolted into facing his awful condition. Remembering his father's house and the better lot of his father's servants, he decided to return home and ask forgiveness.

His father, seeing the boy a great way off, ran to meet him and welcomed him with open arms. He clothed his son, put a ring on his hand, and prepared a feast. While making merry and rejoicing, the father said, "My son was dead, and is alive again; he was lost, and is found" (v. 24).

While all of this was taking place, the older son returned from the fields. When he saw such great rejoicing over his brother who had left home, he became angry and jealous. "Lo, these many years do I serve thee, neither transgressed I at any time thy commandment," he said to his father. "But as soon as this thy son was come, which hath devoured thy living with harlots, thou hast killed for him the fatted calf" (vv. 29-30).

"Son," the father replied, "thou art ever with me, and all that I have is thine. It was meet that we should make merry, and be glad; for this thy brother was dead, and is alive again; and was lost, and is found" (vv. 31-32).

Jesus told this story of "the lost son" along with the parables of "the lost sheep" (15:3-7) and "the lost silver" (15:8-10) to teach that those who are concerned and properly motivated rejoice when the lost is found. They do not criticize the one who shows an interest in the sinner. Here also we see several spiritual principles for the Christian home.

First, *even in a Christian home a child may wander from the straight and narrow way.* The prodigal grew dissatisfied with life as it was. Perhaps given almost all he ever needed and wanted, he still became unhappy. He wanted to be on his own and free from his father's rule.

How illustrative of some Christian youth today! Brought up in Christian homes, sheltered from the evils of the world, they sometimes lose perspective. How easy it is to become so familiar with our heritage that we fail to appreciate what we have.

But like the prodigal, those who are truly Christian and get a taste of the world soon realize its emptiness, its cruelty, and the ensuing heartaches that come in rebellion against God and parents. Thank God, not all become prodigals, nor do they sink as low as he before they regain their spiritual equilibrium. But it does happen, and it pays to be prepared.

Second, *parents should rejoice at true repentance and grant forgiveness.* What a beautiful example of true parental love is seen in the story of the lost son. There was no bitterness on the part of the father, no "I told you so," and no planned rejection to teach a lesson. Nothing heals wounds so quickly, nor reestablishes rapport so well as true and honest forgiveness. The lesson had been learned. There was no need for a "fatherly sermon," no need to say "never let it happen again." A demonstration of true love covered a multitude of sins (1 Pe 4:8).

Third, *children who keep the "letter of the law" and seemingly obey every parental command are not necessarily the more spiritual.* This was true of the son who came from the field. He was angry and jealous. Perhaps his motives for obedience were eventually to cash in on a greater inheritance or to gain a favored position with his father. Whatever his motives, their results were flashed on the screen when his brother returned. True love and concern were missing!

E. A Case of Family Dishonesty

The story of Ananias and Sapphira (recorded in Ac 5:1-11) describes a husband and wife who cooperatively sinned against God and consequently suffered severe judgment.

What was this sin? It was not that they refused to contribute. They could have withheld everything and still not have sinned (Ac 5:4). The plan was voluntary with no obligation for anyone to follow Barnabas' example (4:36-37).

Further, their sin was not that they had held back part of the money. After they had sold the property, they could have done what they pleased.

Rather, their sin was that they were pretending to give

all when they were only giving a part. It was an act of deceit, of dishonesty—a lie before men and to God (5:4).

There is no question about the awfulness of the sin of Ananias and Sapphira. It was wrong and evil! Why God chose to judge them so severely is not ours to question. Rather it is for us to learn that God hates dishonesty.

But perhaps Christians judge Ananias and Sapphira too quickly. It was not primarily the money that was involved, but it was the deception, the attempt to portray something that was untrue. How easy it is in the average home today to practice dishonesty, from the overt act of cheating on income tax reports to the more attitudinal sin of appearing to be something we are not. Christian parents cannot— they dare not—allow dishonesty in any form to creep into their lives. Most children are very perceptive to spot inconsistencies and are not as easily fooled as parents think. Unfortunately they *are* easily disillusioned and confused by double standards.

Perhaps the greatest effects of parental dishonesty are seen in the children and youth who come from such homes. Christian counselors are well aware of how emotionally and spiritually destructive these experiences are. One result is the children's doubt about the reality of Christianity, since they feel they have never seen it work. Others suffer from bitterness, lack of purpose in life, and ambivalent feelings toward their parents and God.

F. Selfish Motives

The event in Matthew 20 involving James and John and their mother illustrates a common happening in family life. There is some question as to the exact details of this story, but one point is clear—all three individuals mentioned were guilty of selfish motives.

Mark tells who prompted the request for positions of

honor in Jesus' kingdom—James and John themselves (Mk 10:35-37). Matthew tells who was convinced that their request was a good idea and was used to approach Jesus for them—their own mother (Mt 20:20-21). The three conspired together to accomplish their selfish desires.

How frequently this same problem occurs in many Christian home today! There are the mother and father who complain that their son or daughter is never given a place of leadership in the youth group. In this way many parents unconsciously reveal their feelings that *they* are not recognized as they should be. Then there are the parents who complain that their children never get an opportunity to sing a solo in the church service.

Of deeper significance is the parent who never admits to himself or anyone else that his child can do wrong—who always takes the child's side, who never sees the child's faults. Frequently this problem is more complex than it appears on the surface, for it may reflect a defense against feelings of failure as a father or mother.

Then there is the scheming parent, perhaps more directly related to the scriptural story in this lesson, who devises means whereby his child may get a decided advantage over others.

Another type of selfish motive on the part of parents is most subtle of all because it can involve self-deception (Jer 17:9-10). This problem may be seen in parents who push their children forward at a very early age in order to demonstrate their unusual talents so the parents may gain recognition *through* their children.

When parents or their children become guilty of behavior prompted by selfish motives, the results can be devastating. Usually the opposite of what was desired happens. When the other disciples discovered the scheming of James and John and their mother, "they were moved with indignation against the two brethren" (Mt 20:24). Not only did James and John *not* get the desired position, but they became objects of hostility and jealousy.

But what are some other results? Parents who complain that their children are being neglected or given secondary positions automatically build into the children various negative motives, depending on the personality structure of the child. In some, there may be feelings of rejection and inferiority. In others, there may be feelings of resentment and hostility. In still others, there may be feelings of uncomfortableness and guilt and eventual resentment toward their parents.

The parent who never admits that his son or daughter can do wrong also creates problems for the child. Most children know when they have done wrong, even though their father and mother may not. Consequently they may lose respect for their parents' judgment. Even more dangerous, however, the child may become convinced he cannot make a mistake or, if he knows he has, he may develop the same protective mechanism demonstrated by his parents—he will not admit it.

Another result can come from what may be innocent parental behavior. When parents push little children forward to demonstrate their abilities and talents, whether for self-satisfaction, or as a ministry, or both, there may be negative results. Since a small child's ego structure is still being formed, he may come to depend on public performance and the applause and praise of men to provide motivation for living. Unless life provides this type of continued experience, it can result in extreme frustration, anxiety, and maladjustment and may even cause the person to find this type of satisfaction in the world if he does not receive it in a Christian environment.

FOR GROUP DISCUSSION AND INTERACTION

1. You will note that jealousy pervades most of these biblical examples. Why is this such a problem in family relationships? What can be done to keep this problem from arising?
2. What other problems, obvious in these biblical examples, plague the Christian home today?

GROUP PROJECTS

Divide into five groups and assign one group to each of the biblical examples. Have each group (1) apply the truth from each example to a modern day situation in the Christian home, (2) suggest causes for the problem, and (3) suggest solutions.

12

SPECIAL FAMILY PROBLEMS

A. Family Morality

THE SITUATION referred to in 1 Corinthians 5:1-5 is not the first reference in the Bible to immorality within the family (see Gen 9:20-25; 19:33-38; 2 Sa 13:1-15). These accounts are included in Holy Writ to reveal the exceeding sinfulness of sin, the human weakness of all mankind. They are never to be cited or dramatized for sensational or evil purposes. In the Old Testament God gave strict laws against such sin, with the severest judgment promised to those who violate His commandments (Lev 20:14, 17). In 1 Corinthians 5 Paul calls for stern church discipline (v. 5). They were not to tolerate this evil practice.

In relatively few instances, we trust, is there immorality in the Christian family such as that prescribed in the above passages. Many cultures, even those that have not been influenced by Christianity, abhor incest and condemn it by law.

But to imagine that the Christian family is immune to intrusions of immoral behavior is only to deny the facts.

More than ever before, the Christian home is under attack from Satan. Great changes in the moral fiber of American society are making their impact upon Christian youth. The philosophy of freedom defined as the "new morality" is infiltrating the thinking of every newspaper-reading, radio-listening, and television-viewing individual. College professors, free-thinking students, journalists, movie producers, and even clergymen are contributing to the spread of this insidious and evil degeneracy which is sweeping the nation.

What does this mean to the Christian parent, to the Christian family? It urgently calls for greater faithfulness in inculcating Christian standards and in building moral character. The laws of God are the same and will endure forever (Ps 119:89). Though the moral customs of society are changing, the moral codes of the Bible will stand the test of time. To violate these absolute, God-given laws will only result in heartache, sorrow, deeper involvement in the sins of the world, and eventual judgment from a Holy God (Gal 6:7-8).

B. Selfishness in Marriage

Individuals who enter into a marirage bond have extensive responsibilities to each other. They are no longer single, no longer able to make decisions separately, or to think or move in any direction without due consideration for the other. "They are no more twain, but one flesh" (Mk 10:8).

However, Christians are still human, under the daily influence of sin, and subject to failure. One of the frequent "fiery darts" Satan flings at marriage partners is the temptation to be selfish. And selfishness can manifest itself in many ways.

In 1 Corinthians 7:1-5, Paul speaks of the most sacred,

most personal, and most intimate relationship of life. Because of its God-ordained design and its ability to bring emotional power, moral strength, and spiritual dynamic to the marriage, it is often the object of great attack from Satan. It may be used by one or the other mate as a weapon to create anxiety, fear, distrust, jealousy, anger, and other hurtful feelings and emotions. It may be used to get even, to display hostility, and to get one's own way.

Those who marry have the sacred responsibility of meeting each other's physical and emotional needs, not withholding what is good and beneficial to the other. Paul says there is one main reason to refrain from "due benevolence" (7:3) and this only by mutual consent. Direct spiritual exercise is the only grounds upon which to arrive at this agreement, and then it is to be only for a season. Otherwise, Satan may take advantage and attempt to lead into sin, either by thought or action (v. 5).

There are other reasons for abstinence, such as illness, bodily weakness, and emotional strain, which should serve as criteria for showing mutual concern, respect, and understanding to the marriage partner. Paul does not treat these factors in this passage, but his total view of the marriage relationships as being like that of Christ and the church implies an attitude of complete unselfishness. How great the need to avoid unjust and selfish demands within the bonds of matrimony.

C. When One Mate Is Unsaved

On numerous occasions one who was not a Christian when married, later receives Christ as Saviour, while the partner continues unbelieving. What then must the Christian husband or wife do?

Some have suggested that in 1 Corinthians 7:12-16 Paul is giving only a personal opinion and not authoritative advice under inspiration of the Holy Spirit (1 Co 7:12). It seems better to understand that verse 10 refers to a statement of Christ recorded in the gospels (Mt 19:3-9), whereas in verse 12 Paul makes his own authoritative statement on a subject not treated by Christ. What Paul suggests here summarizes scriptural teaching. Other biblical authors agree in spirit (see 1 Pe 3:1).

Paul speaks first about "the wife that believeth not" (v. 12). If she wishes to remain with her Christian husband, he should not ask her to leave, nor should he leave her. The same truth applies to "an husband that believeth not" (v. 13). Their marriage is still sacred.

"But," says Paul, "if the unbelieving depart, let him depart" (v. 15). In some instances, an unsaved marriage partner becomes hostile, unbearable and does not wish to remain with the Christian mate. In these cases, the believer should not force the unsaved partner to remain.

But this passage suggests that the Christian mate may be used of God to win the unsaved partner to Christ (v. 16). How may this be done? By continual nagging? By pressure tactics? By spending more time away from the home working in the church? By constantly telling the unsaved person about his lost condition and reminding him that everyone is praying for him?

Not at all! Peter commands wives whose husbands are unsaved to be in subjection to their husbands; that if any obey not the Word of God, they may without a word from the wife be won by her manner of life (1 Pe 3:1-2).

The same principle applies to the Christian husband whose wife is unsaved. He should give her *more* of his time and attention and tenderly reveal the love of Christ through his own life, trusting and praying that she may find his Saviour.

D. Unfaithfulness in Marriage

Unfaithfulness in marriage is an increasing problem in American society and, as with other moral problems, is making its evil impact on the Christian community. The Bible speaks with clarity and force regarding the sin of adultery. It is a work of the sin nature (Gal 5:19), a violation of the holy ordinance of marriage and subject to God's severest judgment (Heb 13:4). It is condemned from Genesis to Revelation, and by no means can it ever be justified. Jesus spoke frequently against this sin, and in the Sermon on the Mount, He clarified the inner moral intent of the law when he labeled inward lust as sinful as the outward act (Mt 5:27-28).

Today many spokesmen for the "new morality" not only advocate the legitimacy of premarital freedom but also extend their philosophy into marriage itself. Even some theologians, ministers, and other religious leaders have opened their minds to the possibility of its justification in certain instances.

No one who believes that the Scriptures are inspired of God and absolute in their teachings can ever regard such a doctrine as acceptable for any marriage partner—saved or unsaved. No one who is aware of the objective findings of scientific psychology and sociology and relates these findings properly to Scripture can deny the ultimate degrading and devastating effects of this philosophy. Only the person who is a victim of his own sinful nature, his own unhappiness, and his own evil desires and rationalizations can excuse such behavior in himself and others.

But though we regard such practice as exceedingly sinful, and scripturally and scientifically unjustifiable, we must remember: "Let him that thinketh he standeth take heed lest he fall" (1 Co 10:12). Failure does not mean there can be no forgiveness. Jesus demonstrated the marvelous grace of God when He said to the adulteress, "Neither do I condemn thee: go, and sin no more" (Jn 8:11). But forgiveness for the repentant one—from God and a loving partner—may never erase the emotional scars. Again we cannot deny the truth of God: man reaps just what he sows (Gal 6:7).

E. The Problem of Divorce

When God created Eve and brought her to Adam, He intended that they would be marriage partners until one of them was removed from this earth by death. Jesus reconfirmed this truth when He quoted Genesis 2:24 to the questioning Pharisees. The fact is that man, by courts of law or any other human ordinance, cannot separate what God has joined. Only the Creator can dissolve this unity, and He has chosen to do it under only two circumstances —fornication (Mt 19:9) or death (Ro 7:2).

In Old Testament times God allowed Moses to "give a writing of divorcement" for other causes. But Jesus quickly clarified this issue to the hypocritical religious leaders of His day when He told them it was allowed only because of the "hardness" of their hearts (Mt 19:8).

Interestingly, the word "cleave" denotes a union of the firmest kind. In the original language it is related to the word meaning "glue" and means to adhere together so firmly that nothing can separate. From the beginning of creation, God did not intend man ever to leave his wife or a wife to leave her husband.

In America today the divorce rate is mounting not only in proportion to the population, but in relationship to the number of marriages. According to recent statistics roughly 400,000 couples are being divorced each year. Christians are not exempt from this problem. Pastors, Christian counselors and other spiritual leaders are facing this tragedy in the lives of Christian people increasingly.

Sociologist Pitirim A. Sorokin comments that the American sex revolution is unparalleled in history and it "is changing the lives of men and women more radically than any other revolution of our time."[1] Wecter adds that "no society in history has shown so widespread a shift in so short a time."[2]

Again the impact of a decadent society is at work undermining the moorings of the Christian church. To let down the bars in the sacred relationship of marriage is to ignore and destroy God's primary plan for human society. To allow the individual units that make up the larger society to disintegrate will eventually help destroy the nation as a whole.

F. The Broken Home

Both Matthew and Mark include the account of Jesus' blessing the little children immediately following His discussion with the Pharisees about divorce (Mt 18:6; 19:13-15). This is interesting in view of the fact that those affected most when a home is broken are the children.

Unfortunately, when parents sin their children suffer. We've already considered the scriptural basis for this (Num 14:18). No sin, it seems, creates as much emotional and spiritual injury as that leading to a broken home. In some cases, children seem to rise above the effects of divorce. But in the majority of cases, there is no doubt that the wounds are deep and lasting.

Why is this true? Of the many emotional needs every child has, one of the greatest is for *security*. The tensions

1. Pitirim A. Sorokin, *The American Sex Revolution* (Boston: Porter Sargent, 1956), p. 4.
2. Dixon Wecter, *Changing Patterns in American Civilization* (Philadelphia: U. of Penn., 1949), p. 17.

and problems leading up to divorce do not contribute to meeting this need. Frequently the atmosphere in the home is filled with hostility, fear, and anxiety, rather than the acceptance, love, and tranquillity which every child needs for adequate spiritual and psychological development.

All parents who are contemplating divorce, even apart from recognizing that this is displeasing to God, should consider the effects on their children. To cause a little one to stumble, to fall, and perhaps to be emotionally crippled for life, is to ask for additional judgment from God. Jesus' actions and feelings toward children seem to imply that the happiness of children is more important than that of adults. Yet when divorce is contemplated, most parents esteem their own happiness of supreme importance.

It should be pointed out, however, that there are those exceptional situations where a hostile, non-Christian partner may create such a bad atmosphere that it would be better to remove the children from the environment. But even in these cases, the Bible teaches that the Christian mate should first attempt through Christ-like behavior to win the unsaved husband or wife to Christ (1 Pe 3:1-2). If this can be done, the *ultimate* results in the lives of the children will be far more beneficial than the *immediate* results of separation.

G. Remarriage

THE WORD OF GOD is clear that marriage is dissolved when one mate dies. The living mate is then free to remarry (1 Co 7:39; Ro 7:3). On the other hand freedom to remarry is not as clearly defined when divorce has transpired on what is called "scriptural grounds."

Some believe the innocent party in a divorce situation is free to remarry. But what is an *innocent* party? Does

God hold guilty only the unfaithful one? What circumstances led to this sinful act? Can one person be completely free from blame and consequently be "innocent"?

Frequently marriage counselors conclude that fault lies on both sides. There is seemingly no completely objective criterion for evaluating who is free from blame. On some occasions, it is clear that the so-called innocent party has not fulfilled the marriage role as taught in Scripture (1 Co 7:3-4) and thus has created temptation for the one who fell (v. 5). Who then is innocent? Who can judge? Who can interpret all the subjective factors which led to the ultimate act of sin? One thing is clear. The one who is personally involved is the most subjective, the most biased, the most capable of unintentionally false conclusions.

These questions are not raised to justify adultery nor to blur the issue. Under all circumstances, no matter what factors led to this sin, it is always wrong. But they are raised to reveal the complex nature of the total problem.

In view of varying opinions and the complex nature of the problem, what advice can be given? To one who is in this predicament and who feels he or she is an innocent party, it becomes an individual responsibility before God. But it must also be remembered that the human heart is deceitful and given over to rationalization (Jer 17:9).

The problems surrounding remarriage should be considered by everyone contemplating marriage. It is vital to seek God's will in this important matter and to enter the bonds of matrimony only after having prayed much about God's choice for a *life* mate, for God wants this step to be for *life*.

FOR GROUP DISCUSSION AND INTERACTION

CASE STUDY

Susan Jones became a Christian as a result of a home Bible

study. Her husband Jim is not yet a Christian. Susan is very excited about her faith. In fact, she spends most of her waking hours attending Bible classes, going to church, and talking to other Christians on the telephone.

One of her main concerns is Jim. He is growing more resentful toward Christianity—the opposite of what she had hoped would happen.

Do you have any advice to give Susan?

INDIVIDUAL OR GROUP ASSIGNMENT

Have each member of the group (or a group working together) select one of the problems mentioned in this chapter and write a realistic case study illustrating it. Select several of these case studies and present them to the group for discussion and solutions.

13

CLOSING THOUGHTS

A. The Home and Christian Service

THE HOME is a *place for Christian fellowship*. During the days of the early church, special buildings had not been erected to serve as meeting places. Rather, Christians went from house to house and met in homes for fellowship and service (Ac 2:46). As the gospel spread, those who were converted seemingly opened their homes on a more permanent basis. On several occasions, Paul spoke of "the church" that met in various private dwellings (Ro 16:5; Col 4:15; Phile 2).

With the introduction of church buildings as meeting places for Christians, perhaps an important ministry was somewhat lost. The informality and warmth of the home can serve as a valuable means for getting to know other Christians on a personal basis and for experiencing the closeness of Christian fellowship that is so necessary for Christian growth.

Many pastors and Christian leaders are utilizing this early biblical pattern to supplement the ministry of the church. Bible studies, prayer groups, and socials are scheduled in various homes as a part of the total church program. This is commendable and should be encouraged. It is especially valuable for new Christians who can so easily be lost in the crowd at church.

The home is also a *place for Christian witness.* The home should be a means for reaching the unsaved. Today there is an increased interest in reaching neighbors and friends for Christ. Many Christian wives and mothers open their homes for informal Bible studies designed especially for non-Christians. Some are utilizing Moody Institute of Science films to reach their next door neighbors who are sometimes classified as "untouchables."

Jesus was often criticized for eating and drinking with "publicans and sinners." His response? "They that are whole have no need of the physician, but they that are sick" (Mk 2:16-17). Christian families need to remind themselves of Jesus' words and also the admonition in Proverbs: "Withhold not good from them to whom it is due, when it is in the power of thine hand to do it" (Pr 3:27).

B. Love—the Key to Success

In today's society, no word is used more frequently when speaking of human relationships than "love." But "love" as defined by the world generally means far less than what Paul meant when he said, "The greatest of these is love" (1 Co 13:13, ASV[1]).

What is love—*true Christian love?* Asking this question is similar to asking someone to define "mental health." No single word or brief definition can explain it! For example, to define "mental health," one must refer to a number of

1. American Standard Version (1901).

related characteristics that form a profile of an individual who is mentally healthy. C. B. Eavey refers to sixteen such characteristics, including a feeling of acceptance, adaptability, a sense of adequacy, courage, happiness, insight, and security.[2]

In 1 Corinthians 13 Paul mentions a series of personality characteristics which form a composite picture of true Christian love. First, however, he contrasts love with gifts and abilities which are not necessarily a manifestation of love in themselves. It is possible that one may have the gifts of speaking, of prophecy, of great understanding, knowledge, and faith, and still not have love. It is possible for an individual to give away everything he has and actually suffer martyrdom, without the presence of love (vv. 1-3).

What then is love? Probably one of the most condensed and positive descriptions of Paul's statements in verses 4-7 is found in what Henry Drummond has called the "spectrum of love." This spectrum includes nine ingredients: patience, kindness, generosity, humility, courtesy, unselfishness, good temper, guilelessness, and sincerity.[3] When these characteristics are present in the life of a Christian, Paul says he is manifesting "love."

Love as defined in the Word of God is the key to a happy and blessed Christian home. Where there is patience and kindness there is response. Where there is generosity there is love in return. Where there is humility there is respect. Where there is courtesy and unselfishness there is happiness. Where there is good temper there is no tendency to bitterness. Where there is guilelessness and sincerity there is trust. Such is the fruit of the Spirit.

2. C. B. Eavey, *Principles of Mental Health for Christian Living* (Chicago: Moody, 1956), pp. 59-74.

3. Henry Drummond, *The Greatest Thing in the World* (London: Collins, n.d.), pp. 32-33.

C. Proper Words

The proper use of words is more important than many realize. Adequate communication is basic to any successful human relationship—whether in business, social life, or in the home. But it is particularly true in the home, for the more closely knit the social structure the more demand there is for skillful communication.

God's Word suggests that proper words can help to achieve Christian goals for the home.

Right words are forcible (Job 6:25). When chosen carefully they make an impact on the listener. They penetrate deeply into the heart. Thoughtless or false words can cause misunderstanding, resentment, and breakdown in communication.

Pleasant words are emotionally strengthening (Pr 16:24). They are like a "honeycomb, sweet to the soul, and health to the bones." They can provide motivation for living and can drive clouds from a dreary sky. A single word of appreciation and kindness can change the day's outlook.

Fitly spoken words are beautiful (Pr 25:11). They are like "apples of gold in pictures of silver." As the eye is captured by a lovely scene, so the ear listens to words that are appropriately spoken. They are captivating and inspiring.

Wise words can be unforgettable (Ec 12:11). They not only penetrate the heart but are fastened in the memory and continue to serve as a guiding light through life.

Words spoken in season are encouraging (Is 50:4). For one who is weary, exhausted, and ready to fall, just a single word can provide encouragement enough to sustain him through a particular trial or problem.

Softly spoken words can turn away anger (Pr 15:1).

How easy it is to respond to angry words with angry words. But an opposite response, one that is kind, a soft word from the heart, is disarming, therapeutic, and powerful in quieting the troubled spirit.

In all these verses lie deep and wonderful truths for the Christian husband, wife, parent, or child. Words properly used open new doors to communication, tap deep resources in the human breast, and create opportunities for fellowship and closeness never before experienced.

D. A Safe Guide

Being a husband or wife, a father or mother is an awesome responsibility. Jesus warned that blind leaders cannot lead the blind, for they will "both fall into the ditch" (Lk 6:39). Parents who themselves do not know the way to go will certainly not be able to lead their children in right and proper paths.

Magazines and newspapers are filled with articles telling how to be a good parent. Each year more books are published treating the subject of interpersonal relationships in the family. Some of the information presented has grown out of careful scientific study and offers helpful suggestions. Other ideas are superficial and harmful. Some psychological doctrines proposed today will be contradicted tomorrow.

Those who rely on man's knowledge alone for direction become confused. But those who look to God's Word as recorded in the Holy Scriptures will find an absolute standard, a divinely inspired Book, with never changing propositions. Therefore every Christian parent must study the Word of God carefully and use the teachings of Scripture to test the findings of this scientific age.

When Moses called Israel together to instruct them before they entered the promised land, he said, "Hear, O

Israel, the statutes and judgments which I speak in your ears this day, that ye may learn them, and keep, and do them" (Deu 5:1).

Christian parents who wish to be successful in administering their homes must do the same. The Word of God must be *learned, kept,* and *practiced.* As they attempt to teach the Scriptures to their children, they need to follow the divine pattern as exemplified by Ezra who "prepared his heart to seek the law of the LORD, and to do it, and to teach in Israel statutes and judgments" (Ezra 7:10).

The Word of God is a safe guide! It will not fail. It serves not only as a source of spiritual food for Christian growth and maturity but also as a divine guide in administering the Christian home. In following its precepts and principles we will find "good success" (Jos 1:8).

For Group Discussion and Interaction

Study carefully 1 Corinthians 13:4-6. Note that love is defined not as an emotion (something we feel) but as an attitude and action (something we do). For example, "love is patient" and "love is also kind."

This runs counter to the superficial definition of love so prevalent in today's society. In fact, what is classified as love today can actually be selfishness, that is, when a person "feels a desire" toward someone, it can be a motive to gratify a personal need. (This, of course, is not *necessarily* wrong.)

How can a Christian keep the proper perspective on love? How can a person know when he is really motivated by love toward others rather than by selfish "love"?

SELECTED BIBLIOGRAPHY

Brandt, Henry R. *Keys to Better Living for Parents*. Chicago: Moody Bible Institute, 1962. (Moody Correspondence Course)

Brandt, Henry R., and Dowdy, Homer E. *Building a Christian Home*. Wheaton, Ill.: Scripture Press, 1960.

Dobson, James. *Dare to Discipline*. Wheaton, Ill.: Tyndale, 1970.

Drakeford, John W. *The Home: Laboratory of Life*. Nashville: Broadman, 1965.

Edens, David, and Edens, Virginia. *Why God Gave Children Parents*. Nashville: Broadman, 1966.

Evans, Laura Margaret. *Hand in Hand: Mother, Child and God*. Westwood, N.J.: Revell, 1960.

Feucht, Oscar E. *Ministry to Families*. St. Louis: Concordia, 1963.

Feucht, Oscar E., ed. *Helping Families Through the Church*. Rev. ed. St. Louis: Concordia, 1971.

Heynen, Ralph. *The Secret of Christian Family Living*. Grand Rapids: Baker, 1965.

Matthews, Charles A. *The Christian Home*. Cincinnati: Standard, n.d.

Narramore, Clyde M. *How to Succeed in Family Living*. Glendale, Calif.: Regal, 1968.

———. *How to Understand and Influence Children*. Grand Rapids: Zondervan, 1957.

Scudder, C. W. *The Family in Christian Perspective*. Nashville: Broadman, 1962.

Small, Dwight H. *Design for Christian Marriage*. Westwood, N.J.: Revell, 1959.

Tournier, Paul. *To Understand Each Other*. Richmond, Va.: John Knox, 1962.

Zuck, Roy B., and Getz, Gene A. *Ventures in Family Living*. Chicago: Moody, 1971.